Emotional Stimulus Package™

Your Guide to Re-creating the American Dream

By

The Lemonade Network, LLC

Andrea C. Skelly, Ph.D., MPH

Catherine Lidster, GCFP

Danny Fitzpatrick, MPA

Jeanette Carter

Kathy Pandich

Marsha Stopa, APP

First published by Dog Ear Publishing
4010 W. 86th Street, Ste H
Indianapolis, IN 46268
www.dogearpublishing.net

dog ear
PUBLISHING

ISBN: 978-160844-239-3
Library of Congress Control Number: 2009942052

This book is printed on acid-free paper.

Printed in the United States of America

The information and concepts presented by The Lemonade Network, LLC are for educational purposes only. We do not diagnose, treat, prevent or cure any disease or condition. Our program is not intended to substitute for the advice, treatment and/or diagnosis of a qualified medical professional.

Table of Contents

Identifying specific issues helps break the
numbness of disbelief.

Working through these intense emotions
reclaims your power.

Releasing anger is necessary to maintain health,
relationships and continued progress.

Observing feelings and behavior leads to new ways
of thinking and reacting.

Acknowledgements

The members of the Lemonade Network thank our families and friends for their support, understanding and encouragement while we poured our hearts into this book. It has been a cathartic journey and growing experience that brought together six virtual strangers who are now friends, colleagues and business partners. Each author brings a unique perspective and contribution to the book and The Lemonade Network.

We are indebted to the people who have allowed us to write about their personal stories. The authentic power of this book lies in these stories about real people, their struggles and the choices they have made. While several brave individuals did grant us permission to use their full names, we have decided that because many of these struggles are ongoing, we prefer to use first names to protect their privacy. Many thanks to Adam, Andrea, Carol, Cathy, Chris, Jerry, Jon, Wanda, Kathy, Marsha and Mary.

Our thanks to everyone who reviewed the book and provided invaluable feedback that made the final product significantly better: Leisha Bell, Patty Fish, Robert Giordano, Sue Grab, Ian Gullion, Lora Inman, Sandy Langelier, Jessica Lester, Ruth Lidster, Aaron Manning and Cindy Tolbert.

We especially thank Debbie Schroeder, our teacher and coach, for her insight, help, guidance and support.

Introduction

You could call it serendipity or you could simply call it a great, timely idea waiting to be born.

Emotional Stimulus Package is an idea whose time has come.

If you or someone close to you is experiencing the pain of losing your American Dream, this book offers guidance to help navigate your way out of the forest and back into the sunshine.

Emotional burdens are often the result of financial or other difficult life challenges. Those challenges may be caused by the loss of a job, looming foreclosure or bankruptcy, or watching that slow-growing nest egg wiped out almost overnight. The emotional toll often manifests as serious effects on physical health.

In each chapter, you will find a story – some excruciatingly personal, some that may truly resonate with your pain, or some that simply resemble the situation of someone you know. The stories in *Emotional Stimulus Package* are real stories about real people. You may be able to relate to one or more of these stories and benefit from the ways the individuals worked through their unplanned and unwelcome crises.

The authors' objective in this book is to help people deal with their emotional struggle and move toward recreating their dream. Parallels are drawn with the stages of grief. Through the stories, questions and exercises throughout the book, you will acquire tools and knowledge to help you on your journey

Emotional Stimulus Package is not a clinical or academic book. It is a book of practical information and suggestions to help readers take a more positive and proactive approach to their situation.

The six authors of this book, each of whom brings years of experience in various counseling and coaching fields, have a desire to make an even greater impact on others' lives. Their own experiences and awareness of the physical impacts of stress led each of them to learn more about the specialized area of health coaching. It was in this arena they met.

One important thing the authors have in common is a passion to help individuals take a realistic look at their circumstances, evaluate what is preventing them from overcoming their challenges and emerge victorious with a better life.

In defining their mission, the well-known Dale Carnegie phrase "When life hands you lemons, make lemonade" kept surfacing. It seemed natural their name should be **The Lemonade Network**. It is from this platform the authors offer their experience and guidance.

In the biographies provided at the back of the book you will see how the authors of *Emotional Stimulus Package* have a passion for helping others. They live in six different states from coast to coast and, as of this writing, have not met face to face. It was an amazing coordinated effort by virtual strangers with different backgrounds, life experiences, marital status, education and previous professions.

In their more than 300 total years of life, the group has navigated a vast range of challenges and experiences that provide a collaborative wisdom from which they draw.

As a group, they have survived many things including: eight job firings or layoffs, seven bankruptcies or severe financial difficulties, five tax liens or audits, one foreclosure and one mortgage default, seven divorces, six losses of assets through poor decisions or misguided investments, five failed businesses, the loss of 19 close loved ones, eight unexpected instances of significantly reduced income, the raising of nine children, six serious life-changing illnesses for themselves or close family, five "bosses from hell," one home lost to fire and an average loss of more than 50 percent of life savings and investments in the current economic downturn.

All have come through with a new knowledge of themselves, a new level of confidence and a deep desire to help guide others through the maze from victim to victor. It is their hope you will find in this collection of stories and tools, ones that resonate with your situation. It is their passion to provide information, guidance and methods that uniquely address your needs.

The intent of this volume is to help you personally evaluate where you are in the process and provide assessments and exercises to help you work through the process from whatever current point you find yourself. There is a Resources section at the end of this book you can use as a guide for more information. We suggest you review the additional tools and materials provided by The Lemonade Network for more guidance.

Take the time to sincerely work through this book and the available support material. You will emerge at the other end having made measurable progress in recovering from the emotional impact of your experience.

Are you tired of struggling and getting nowhere? Are your emotions locked in a continual "down" mode? Do you feel like you're drowning?

Are you ready for a change in your attitude and outlook? Ready to turn the corner and see what is there for you?

What are the risks of staying where you are? What will your life be like next year if you continue doing what you're currently doing?

What are the benefits of getting your life back in order? Imagine for a moment how different your life could be if you had the tools and the encouragement to take one step at a time down the road to the recovery of your American Dream.

An extensive toolkit of options is available to guide you on your journey. In addition to the *Emotional Stimulus Package* book, workbook and workshops, individual and group coaching services are available from each of the six Lemonade Network coaches through www.LemonadeNetwork.com.

Are you ready to take that first step? Imagine yourself reaching out and taking the collective hand of the authors who will be your guides on the journey.

Shall we begin?

CHAPTER 1

Grieving the Death of the American Dream

The illusion dies so something deeper can take its place.
~Joan of Arcadia episode

Over the past few years, the United States and for that matter the world, has seen the collapse of the financial system as we have come to know it in the past 70 years or more. We've witnessed a death: The death of the American Dream.

You have your own version of the American Dream. Perhaps it is to purchase your first home. Maybe your dream is to buy a brand new car instead of an old unreliable used car. The dream may be of a well-kept garden and home with two cars, 1.5 children, a cat and a dog. The dream of a reasonably comfortable lifestyle, a paid-off mortgage or the promise of retirement. The dream of job security. Now dead. Gone. And it will never be the same.

Death is a fact of life. We will all experience the death of a loved one at some point in our lives. If not an actual death, by early adulthood most of us have experienced a loss of some kind. We've weathered the break up of a significant relationship or survived an incapacitating illness, which are more metaphorical "deaths." At first we can't believe they are gone and may go so far as to deny that they will no longer be with us. Then the pain and guilt sink in as we realize that they are gone and we become consumed with all of the things we think we "woulda, coulda, shoulda" done while they were alive and we feel guilty.

We become angry at anything and everything. Perhaps we set up bargaining sessions with ourselves, God or our concept of the Divine as we resist the changes we know we need to make. As we reflect, we may become isolated and depressed and find it difficult to move on.

Then there is a turning point – a thought, a situation, an inspiration – that gets us to thinking that maybe, just maybe, we *can* see and do things differently. This, in turn, allows us to begin to re-create our lives without the loved one. We begin to work through the issues and plan a new beginning. As we accept and prepare to continue with our lives, we find new hope for the future.

Individually and collectively as a nation, we are going through the same grieving process over the death of our American Dream, whatever that means to us personally. Like the grieving process related to the loss of a loved one, we must work through the stages in order to get to the other side. There is no way out, but we can make choices as we work through the stages.

This collapse has not been just financial, it has been personal. While there is obviously a component of financial recovery that is needed, the emotional recovery is as (or perhaps more) important if we are to re-create a dream for our nation and ourselves.

In Chinese, the word *crisis* is composed of two characters: one that represents danger and the other, opportunity. So, translated it means that crisis is a "dangerous opportunity." While it is natural for us to react to the danger, there is the risk that the reaction masks potential opportunities. Crisis can provide an important kick in the pants for us to make necessary changes so we can look for and explore these new situations.

As part of the current crisis, we have lost sight of what is truly valuable and how our distinct talents may allow us to make unique contributions. Working through the stages of grief may help us find the inner resources to make the necessary changes and take advantage of opportunities created by the current crisis.

This is a call to a new consciousness, a call to re-evaluate who we really are and where our self-worth and true wealth come from personally and as a nation. It is a call to create a new type of abundance, which yes, can contain financial wealth and can encompass so much more. We have the opportunity to create a new culture and a new paradigm around true wealth and abundance by first creating it in ourselves. It is a call to take the chance and have the courage to move forward!

Any crisis is also a call to make new choices. The old paradigm will no longer work. This book is about choice and change. It is about seeking a new blueprint for creating a meaningful life. It is about taking the chance that the new blueprint may be better than the old one. It is a book about YOU and about us and how, individually and collectively, we can re-create the American Dream.

The purpose of this book is to help you recognize and use the stages of grief as steppingstones on the path to rebuilding your American Dream. Working through these stages will help you lay a solid foundation on which to rebuild. So this book is also about hope! Building the foundation and getting new tools along your journey will allow you to take control and shape your future.

Here are the stages and a sample of the things you'll learn as you work through the chapters.

- **Stage 1: Shock and denial** may have you numbed in disbelief. You'll have the opportunity to break free from this stage by specifying the issues and their impact.

- **Stage 2: Pain and guilt** set in as you acknowledge what is going on. Learning to reclaim your power by working through these emotions gives you an important lesson on your journey.

- **Stage 3: Anger and bargaining** are common as we put the pain and guilt behind us. In order to maintain our health and relationships and continue progressing on the path, they need to be released. We offer some practical solutions for recognizing these masks and removing them.

- **Stage 4: Depression, reflection and loneliness** often follow anger and bargaining. As you reflect on the magnitude of your situation, it is normal to feel stuck, overwhelmed, discouraged and isolated. By observing your feelings and behavior patterns and considering new ways of thinking and reacting, you'll gain insights into how to put this stage behind you.

- **Stage 5: The upward turn** is a vulnerable and fragile time, as we turn and begin to climb out of the depths of pain, denial, anger and depression, accepting what was while focusing on the future with a new perspective.

- **Stage 6: The reconstruction stage** gives you the opportunity to redefine your situation and reconnect with your inner assets to set a direction for additional action. You add more tools to rebuild your dream.

- **Stage 7: Acceptance and hope** emerge as you make use of the steppingstones laid in the previous stages. Ideas for continued action are combined with methods for tapping into a new sense of inner peace and joy as you anticipate good times again.

Although the stages are listed in a given order, in reality you may spend some time weaving in and out of stages more than once. Although the path may twist and turn, as long as you keep doing the work, you'll keep moving up and out of your grief. You may move quickly through some stages and need to spend more time in others. That is fine! This is not a race, but a journey that cannot be rushed.

Regardless of where you start, the chapters provide food for thought and ideas for working through to the next stage. As you learn what you need to learn from each stage, you will find that your toolkit for rebuilding is substantial and your confidence and hope gain momentum. While moving through the stages may not be anyone's idea of fun, it is the only way to the other side. You can do it and we are here to help.

Throughout the book, there are questions for consideration and exercises that are based on principles for successful change that the authors and others have used to move past personal crisis. It is our hope that you will:

- Be able to identify where you are in the grieving process
- Realize it is okay to grieve the loss, natural to go through the stages and there is a light at the end of the tunnel
- Create small steps you can take to move through the stages and lay a solid foundation for rebuilding your dreams

This is a very personal journey and, although our intent is to provide as much information and assistance as we can, for some, the book is perhaps only a beginning. For those who are motivated and interested in "going for the gold" and accelerating their movement along the path toward a new dream, The Lemonade Network has a number of tools and resources, many of which can be tailored and personalized to correspond to your needs and goals. Visit our website at www.LemonadeNetwork.com for details about options which may best fit your needs.

You have a choice. We all do. We can let a crisis crush us or, like the phoenix, rise out of the ashes to fly once again, perhaps along a different path to a different destination. The path will have its challenges, but if we don't take the chance, we miss the opportunity to discover the new destination that may be much better than the one that has passed away.

And when you get the choice to sit it out or dance,
I hope you dance.
~ "I Hope You Dance" by Leeann Womack

CHAPTER 2

Stage 1: Shock and Denial

> **Shock and denial** may have you numbed in disbelief.
> You'll have the opportunity to break free from this stage
> by specifying the issues and their impact.

As you begin the grief process, shock and denial will offer you an altered reality. Initially it will be beneficial as it blocks the pain, but beware of the draw to stay in this stage.

You can't run away from trouble. There ain't no place that far.
~Uncle Remus

Kathy's Story

Kathy rolled over in bed and groaned when she heard the door open to their Vegas hotel room. It was 6:15 a.m. Granted, they were on Eastern Time, but still, she wanted to be able to sleep in. She had left her 9–month-old son with her sister – it was the first time they were apart. It was only three days away from her son, Max, but yesterday she almost booked a flight back after just one day away from him. Kathy's husband convinced her to stick it out for one more day. So this morning, she was lying in bed instead of on a plane.

Kathy mumbled, "Stephen, is that you?" "Yes," he said. "I went down for coffee and the paper. The woman behind the counter said she heard there was a bombing at the Pentagon. She didn't think it was true but turn on the TV. See what's going on."

Kathy turned on the TV and saw smoke coming out of the World Trade Center. She could not believe what was on the screen. This didn't make any sense. She heard what the commentators were saying about the planes but it didn't register in her mind or her body. She held her breath as she watched and waited. Then, she saw the first tower fall. The pain in her chest was intense.

Kathy's brain kicked into gear and all she could think about was not having any phone numbers with her. Where was her friend Rosemarie? Did she get out? Where were her other friends and former colleagues?

Until a year-and-a-half before, Kathy had worked at Cantor Fitzgerald on the 103rd floor of One World Trade. On 9/11 Cantor Fitzgerald lost 658 employees – all of the employees in the office that fateful day.

Ignore the Magnitude

As Kathy and her husband walked into the convention center of the trade show they were attending, people were in groups around the television monitors lining the hall watching the devastation. There was little, almost no conversation.

Yet, as they entered the exhibit hall, they saw people actually conducting business. How could this be? How could anyone think about anything else other than what was happening around the country? And yet, some were explaining how packaging systems worked or the best way to get a box from one end of the warehouse to the other.

Later that day in the sports bar they were surrounded by the big flat screen TVs, all turned to the news. Looking around the room to study the people, Kathy wondered what everyone else was thinking. It wasn't easy to tell. Everyone looked normal. It looked like any other evening at a sports bar except for the pictures on the screens. People were eating, talking and occasionally looking up as if something caught their attention for a brief moment.

Classic denial…

A few very long days later, Kathy's son was back in her arms. She had trouble putting him down even as she picked up the phone to try to find her friend Rosemarie. With tears streaming down her face and a lump in her throat, she called, trying to find her friend. As the phone rang, Kathy was terrified she would reach a family member.

"Hello." Kathy heard a familiar voice. It was Rosemarie! She was alive! She hadn't gone into work that day! Her two little babies still had their mother and her husband still had his wife. There were many miracles that day and she was one of them.

It has been more than eight years since the attacks, the initial shock and denial hopefully long gone. Each American has gone through their grieving process along with the country as a whole and we are a stronger nation because of it.

Once again the nation is reeling from a heavy blow. The economic crisis has affected nearly every American with record layoffs, foreclosures and destruction of retirement funds. The impact of just one of these events can cause an extreme reaction that can initiate the grieving process.

Loss of a ...

In the first stage of grief, shock and denial play an integral role in protecting you from yourself. The shock part of this stage is brief and can include a sense of numbness, disbelief and inability to function. Emotional pain can cut to your very soul. Your brain can temporarily numb that pain until you are mentally and physically ready to deal with reality. You are not necessarily oblivious to what is going on around you but you are able to keep the situation at arm's length. To internalize it at this point is just too painful. Sometimes we may wish that this part would last a bit longer. As the fog lifts, we move into denial. This part can last a lot longer.

It is difficult to deal with extreme change. Most people's lives are routine. Some days may be busier than others with errands, baseball games or other activities. However, the majority will tell you that they live a normal life and their days are predictable.

When an event rocks your world, it is very common to avoid thinking about the situation. Like a deer in the headlights, people avoid making decisions all together. They continue to live their lives as if nothing had happened. It is easier to focus on a particular task at hand. Remember the people at the trade show? They were in Las Vegas for a reason and rather than stop and think about the tragedy, it was easier to immerse themselves in the business of the day.

Denial can sometimes distort our reality. With the actual death of a loved one, you know the loss is permanent and irrevocable. Yet with the death or destruction of a lifestyle, you can initially refuse to believe it is true. Many will continue with their daily activities until the cash or credit simply runs out. Be very careful here. If your head is in the sand, you may miss significant opportunities to help yourself.

The amount of time spent in this stage will vary greatly from one person to the next. There are many factors that play a part in how long you can "hide out." Some people can stay in denial for years until they are forced to face the cold hard truth. For others, it may only be a few short months until they must react.

The stress generated in this stage can lead to many physical ailments including fatigue, headaches, as well as muscle and joint pain. Your brain may be in denial but your body may still show the strain. You are not alone. These feelings are normal. When individuals are confronted with a significant life change, they will experience the grieving process.

Nothing can compare to the loss of a loved one, yet the loss or significant change in one's lifestyle can take an enormous emotional toll.

The denial defense mechanism manifests in different ways for different people as illustrated in the following story.

Chris's Story

Chris desperately hoped that no one noticed his anxiety as they waited for the waiter to bring the bill. For the 100th time that evening, he mentally kicked himself for not double-checking the balance on his credit cards before leaving the house. Which card should he use? He could feel his face getting hot.

He knew his wife, Sally, would be mortified if the waiter brought the bill back and told him the card has been declined. He should have told his friends, Tom and Becky, that he wasn't feeling well tonight and cancelled their dinner reservations. He just needed to get through this month. With next month's commission check, he would be able to get caught up.

Chris handed the waiter the bill and his credit card. He said a silent prayer.

"You're coming on the Caribbean Cruise with us in July, right?" Tom asked.

"Of course, we wouldn't miss it!" Chris answered. The cruise was a little more than three months away. He would put in some overtime and with the extra commission money he should be able to swing it or maybe transfer one of his credit cards to a different company with a higher credit limit.

What was taking the waiter so long? He shouldn't have had another cocktail. How much were they? Finally, Chris saw the waiter walking towards his table. He felt his blood pressure rising. The waiter smiled and handed Chris the credit card receipt. "Oh, thank God!" He picked the right card.

Tomorrow was Saturday. Chris planned to sit down at his desk and sort through the bills. Or maybe he would clean out the garage first…

Chris needed to regain control of his life and yet he was in denial. He continued to slide from one month to another, ignoring the warning signals and avoiding the truth.

This same story is playing out across the country. The game has changed and the players have yet to understand the new rules in this uncertain economy. We are left in a state of confusion.

Let's say you've worked all of your life at the same company. It is basically a second home. Your friends are there; you have lunch with them every day. There are barbeques on the weekends. Your sons play baseball together. Today is the day they hand you the pink slip.

Maybe your dream of owning a home had finally come true. You slaved over the lawn, pulling weeds, fertilizing, trimming and mowing. It was fun arguing over just the right shade of paint for the dining room. It didn't matter that you didn't have any fingernails left after tearing off the last piece of wallpaper. Today is the day the bank called with the notice of foreclosure.

You can't believe this is happening to you! *Shock.*

There has to be a mistake! *Denial.*

The key is to recognize the signs of denial in order to move past it so you can begin to recover.

It took Chris almost a year of juggling bills, avoiding collection calls and sliding on mortgage payments until he finally acknowledged the severity of his situation. He contacted a credit counselor to begin his journey to financial recovery as well as a life coach to help him work through the emotional wounds.

Are you talkin' to ME?

Are you in denial? This first stage is a tricky one. It may be hard to admit at first.

Read the following questions and answer them honestly. They may help you admit where you are right now, which is the first step in moving forward.

- Have you ever jumped up and screamed, "Don't answer it!" when the phone rang because you thought it might be a credit card company on the other end?
- Are you going out to dinner every other night and charging it on a credit card?
- Are you planning a vacation and calculating which five credit cards to take with you based on the available balances?
- Do you toss and turn at night because you won't let your mind settle on the current state of your finances?

- Are you reading romance novels or thrillers instead of non-fiction books that address your situation?

If you answered yes to any of these questions, you may be in some form of denial.

Insights

You have started the grieving process. We discussed how Shock and Denial can initially provide a critical coping mechanism and how some people may try to "hide out" in this stage. Let's summarize.

- Chris waited almost a year to acknowledge the severity of his situation. He had lost many opportunities during that time that could have softened the economic blow. Don't wait to face the truth. Don't miss those opportunities.
- It is frightening to admit you have a problem because your life is going to change. You *will* move forward, experience road-blocks and deal with a multitude of emotions. Keep your eye on the horizon and your goals. It will be worth the trip.
- The reality is: The sooner you start, the sooner you will reach your destination.

Exercises

Admit you have a problem. It sounds simple, right? But that doesn't mean it is easy. You've worked hard, you did what you thought you should do, the way you thought you should do it. Here comes the "but," *but* it didn't work out that way. Acknowledge that it didn't work so you can move forward. Take a moment to sit down in a quiet place and think about the following questions.

1. How has my life deviated from my plan?
2. What adjustments do I need to make so I will be happy with my life?
3. How is my family affected by my current circumstances?

Moving On

How do these questions make you feel? Once reality sets in and you truly absorb the full impact of your current circumstances, you need to be aware of the pain that will follow. The pain will come. It will not be easy but know that with pain comes movement. The movement is forward. You are entering the next stage of grief, which is Pain and Guilt.

Read the following chapters to find out how to deal with these feelings and many others. We will walk through this process together. If you find yourself struggling along the way, visit us at www.LemonadeNetwork.com to find out more about individual coaching and how it can help.

CHAPTER 3

Stage 2: Pain & Guilt

Pain and guilt set in as you acknowledge what is going on. Learning to reclaim your power by working through these emotions gives you an important lesson on your journey.

If you're going through hell, keep going.
~Winston Churchill

If you have successfully transitioned from the previous stage of grief, you will most likely be experiencing a tremendous amount of pain, the very feeling you were suppressing and denying. Although it may not seem like it now, this is a positive sign. It means you are progressing. The pain could be rooted in guilt over decisions you have made or not made in your journey to this point. Life feels uncertain and scary during this phase.

Having worked through some of the exercises in the previous chapter, you may now be ready to address your situation and the pain involved. The important thing is to *acknowledge* the pain. It serves no purpose to hide or deny it. We've already seen how that can be detrimental to your health and well-being. So the question remains, what do you do with it?

Carol's Story

Carol was well on her way to being set for life. She had a series of career advancements in the area of arts administration, was well respected in the community and was earning a comfortable six-figure income. She had a dream home complete with sauna, Jacuzzi, swimming pool and enviable gardens. All was just as she had envisioned and planned.

Until one day when it all came crashing down.

Because of internal political machinations, Carol and her boss were eliminated from their positions. Yes, fired! How could this be? In a flash, her reputation was compromised and she could no longer find work in her chosen profession.

Being the creative, resourceful person that she was, Carol began to reinvent herself. She always had an interest in real estate and decided to try her hand in that potentially lucrative field. The way she figured it, she had nothing to lose and everything to gain. But things didn't work out as planned. Nobody expected the tremendous housing crash, especially Carol. She was accustomed to being successful in her professional endeavors. This newfound "failure" was new territory for her.

Her embarrassment at not being successful in her career turned to pain. She was utterly humiliated. The humiliation then turned to guilt. She assumed her lack of success must be because she wasn't working hard enough or smart enough. She began to feel guilty for not calling more people, guilty for not sitting in the office more hours, guilty for not going door-to-door, guilty for not sending postcards, guilty for not spending more on her marketing campaign.

Guilty for getting fired. Guilty for getting herself in this mess. You name it. It was all Carol's fault! It never occurred to her that her plight was part of a bigger picture in the current economic environment.

Guilt: It's All My Fault!

When Carol recognized her self-image was so utterly wrapped around her career she sought the help of a life and wellness coach. She wanted her self-esteem back. She knew the pain and guilt were no longer serving her but she needed help in moving through them.

Carol was already a step ahead of the game. She was aware of her pain and was feeling it for all it was worth. She and her coach worked on naming the pain and releasing it. Then they went to work on the guilt.

The guilt was a little more difficult to release. After all, if Carol's "failure" wasn't her fault, whose fault was it? The important thing to remember here is *it doesn't matter whose fault it was!* What's done is done. You may have made decisions in the past you now regret. Some external circumstance may have landed you a low blow. Someone may have done you an injustice.

The point is all that's in the past. What's important now, and the only thing worth spending your effort on, is the now. The decisions you make now will shape your future. You have the choice to let go of the things you can't control or fix them and move on. You will not, and cannot, change the past but you can let go of it. You can handle whatever challenges life throws your way. You will.

Without a doubt, the most important thing to remember and practice when it comes to guilt is forgiveness. Of course, that is easier said than done. There are a number of emotional releasing techniques available to help you through this process. Carol tried several before finding the combination that felt most comfortable for her. You may discover some work better than others for you, too. Take a look at the Resources section in the back of this book to find more information about emotional releasing techniques. Try them out. See which ones work best for you.

One day at a time - this is enough. Do not look back and grieve over the past, for it is gone: and do not be troubled about the future, for it has not yet come. Live in the present, and make it so beautiful that it will be worth remembering.
~Ida Scott Taylor

Jon and Wanda's Story

Jon and Wanda found a nice house in the country. Although they both earned modest salaries in the healthcare industry, the real estate agent assured them they would be able to afford the house payments. They found a mortgage plan that gave them an affordable monthly payment for five years, followed by a balloon payment of $70,000. The agent said not to worry and suggested they could sell or refinance in five years. All was good, for five years. Then the $70,000 was due and they had a hard time refinancing. They decided to retire at the same time, which reduced their monthly income.

After much difficulty, they finally got the refinancing approved and everything was copasetic for a while. Then, according to the terms of the new loan, the monthly payments went up at the same time that Jon's retirement incentive ceased, meaning he received yet another cut in pay!

The bills were mounting. Eventually, the couple stopped paying the mortgage. Their relationship was on the rocks. Wanda suffered a stroke. Jon went into a severe depression. The foreclosure date was set. They would lose it all – including their health.

When Guilt looks like Blame

Jon and Wanda's sad story is an example of what can happen when we never get through the Shock and Denial stage. As we learned in the previous chapter, serious health ramifications can be the result. And that's exactly what happened. Although they knew they faced a reduction in income, the couple never adjusted their lifestyle accordingly. They continued to treat themselves to fancy restaurants, weekend getaways and expensive entertainment without checking to see what their new budget allowed. In fact, they never created a budget. Keeping their heads in the sand, they spent money freely in order to dull the pain of their economic reality.

They then went directly into the guilt and blaming stage. Accusing the real estate agent of double-crossing them, they blamed him for their woes. They blamed the system. They blamed the current economic crisis. They blamed the bank. They blamed each other. There was a lot of blame to go around.

Unfortunately, Jon and Wanda are likely to stay stuck in the blaming game unless they are willing to take responsibility for their actions. Sure, life circumstances were sometimes stacked to their disadvantage. They may even have been victims of a nefarious mortgage fraud. But until they acknowledge their role in the chain of events, they will not learn and grow from the experience. Eventually, they will find themselves back in the same or similar situation. The lesson here is to feel the pain, acknowledge our part and take responsibility. Then (most importantly) forgive ourselves and others.

Adam's Story

When Adam's wife found out we were writing this book, she suggested we interview her husband for one of the stories. He showed up for our interview and immediately apologized for being late, although he did seem to be on time. When coffee and cookies were offered, Adam politely declined, stating he had just started a cleansing procedure and water would be just fine.

Adam managed to find time to meet with us even though he was a real estate agent and running between appointments. He had gotten four new listings and was busy showing them. Our first thought was, "Gee, what are we going to talk to this guy about? He doesn't seem to be affected by the economic downturn at all. Why would his wife suggest we talk with him?"

Then he began his story. As it turned out, Adam hadn't brought in a single dime all year. He felt he was lacking on his end of the bargain and his pride was definitely hurting. Unfortunately, his wife wasn't bringing in much either and they had all they could do to keep the wolf from the door. The mortgage hadn't been paid in six months and the credit card debt was out of control. How is it he remained so upbeat and healthy?

He went on to explain that when he and his wife saw their financial situation heading for a crisis they made an agreement it would not affect their relationship. They talked it through. The first thing they did was sit down and make a list, writing down the worst possible things that could result from their economic plight. When they saw losing their home and getting an apartment might be a realistic outcome, they realized things weren't so bad after all. They could handle that.

Pain vs. Power

Adam knew the value of addressing the wolf at the door face-to-face. By actually looking at the situation and making choices, he was able to ease the pain of his situation. This is not to be confused with ignoring the pain. Adam's pride was hurt and he felt guilty, but by taking action, he granted himself power over the pain.

He made smart choices. He was taking care of his health. He discussed the situation with his wife. They formed a support team with each other. When he discovered 40 percent of the home sales in his area were short sales, he made himself an expert in short sales. Adam's willingness to face reality and make a step-by-step plan got him through the Pain and Guilt stage. He refused to be a victim. He acknowledged the pain. He addressed it and took responsibility. You can, too.

Let me embrace thee, sour adversity,
For wise men say it is the wisest course.
~William Shakespeare

Where Are You?

Did you recognize yourself in any of the three stories? If so, hopefully it was with Carol or Adam's story. What they had in common is that they both acknowledged their pain and sought help. Carol worked through this stage with the help of her coach and Adam sought the support of his wife. This is crucial to your success. There are myriad opportunities for you to get help in this process. Keep in touch with The Lemonade Network by joining our community at www.LemonadeNetwork.com. We'd love to hear from you. Please don't feel that you are alone.

If your situation more closely resembles that of Jon and Wanda, learn from their mistakes. Be realistic. Be willing to acknowledge the pain if it is present. Seek outside help. Don't let the situation negatively affect your health.

Questions for Consideration

Take a look at the statements below. Are you saying any of these things to yourself? Does any of this ring true for you? If so, you may be in the Pain and Guilt stage.

- If only I had put aside more savings like the money management advisors suggested.
- I'm such a disappointment to my spouse. I'm supposed to be the breadwinner around here.
- If only I'd volunteered to work more overtime or not taken my vacation during the busy season.
- I should have understood the mortgage before I signed it. Why did I let myself be talked into such a big house!
- It hurts to look like a loser to my family and friends.
- I shouldn't have gone on that shopping spree!
- If only I hadn't listened to that mortgage broker/real estate agent. He really took advantage of me.
- I should have kissed up to the boss like Joe did. That's why he didn't get laid off.
- I should have seen this coming!

Insights

Getting through the pain and guilt is not easy and there's no guarantee you won't be visiting this stage again. Let's review some of the insights gained in this chapter.

- The first step is to acknowledge the pain. This level of self-awareness is a huge accomplishment. The difficulty in making this breakthrough from the Shock and Denial stage is that, by the nature of our current emotional state, we don't even know that we are in it. Although it may seem counter-intuitive, recognition of the pain is to be welcomed. For now we understand that it is a necessary step toward healing our grief.

- Taking responsibility for our part in the situation frees us from getting bogged down in the blame game. Although we can't always control our outer circumstances, we do have the choice and responsibility to manage our reactions to them. Getting wrapped up in blaming others or outside forces for our situation keeps us spinning in a stagnant loop. A more productive perspective is to view ourselves as a participant in our circumstance rather than a victim or someone it "happened to."

- A possible outcome when accepting responsibility, of course, is to feel a certain amount of guilt. It's imperative that we forgive ourselves for regrettable choices we've made in the past. Whatever is done is done and we now have opportunities to make new and better choices today. Forgiving ourselves and others allows us the freedom to move forward.

Exercises

1. Think back to the previous week. What actions have you taken, or not taken, that put you in a position of power? What choices have you made lately? Maybe you've begun networking for some new business opportunities, or renewing relationships with colleagues and peers. Perhaps you've caught up on those doctor appointments you never seemed to have time for previously.

2. What have you done, or not done, that keeps you on the side of pain? Have you been procrastinating on creating a monthly budget for yourself? Take stock and write it down.

    Example:

Pain	Power
I've avoided going through that big stack of papers and mail on the kitchen table.	I started a spreadsheet accounting for all of my monthly expenses.

3. Sit back, get comfortable. Close your eyes and take a deep breath. Think. What is causing you to feel emotional pain right now? Where in your body do you feel it? Is it in your gut? Your throat? Your heart? What does the pain look like? What color is it? Can you give it a shape? Can you give it a name? What does it sound like? Just be aware of it. Don't try to change it or eliminate it. In fact, don't try and do anything. Simply

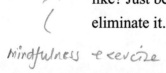

mindfulness exercise

notice it. Do this once a day until the pain is no longer present.

Moving On

Now that you recognize the characteristics and have worked through some of the exercises, it should be less painful should you find yourself here again. You know what to expect and what to do.

If you've truly felt and accepted the pain, you're probably pretty angry about it. Are we right? What did you ever do to deserve this situation? Are you feeling that if only it would go away you will never get yourself in this predicament again? Are you ready to do some bargaining? If so, you are ready to move on to the next stage of grief.

CHAPTER 4

Stage 3: Anger and Bargaining

Anger and bargaining are common as we put the pain and guilt behind us. In order to maintain our health and relationships and continue progressing on the path, they need to be released. We offer some practical solutions for recognizing these as masks and removing them.

The Anger and Bargaining stage has its own set of tricky passages to navigate. This stage offers a two-edged sword. After being lost, often almost paralyzed, in the Shock and Denial stage and then the Pain and Guilt stage, the often explosive energy of anger and deceptive movement of bargaining can be mistaken for taking action.

A healthy release of anger is a step up from fear and can motivate you to action, but many times we bottle up our emotions, until finally releasing them in unhealthy ways, often causing unnecessary pain. Bargaining can be therapeutic in that it helps you try on different versions of reality for a while, giving you time to figure out your options. On the flip side, you also can get caught in a cycle of activity that accomplishes little while you anxiously tread water.

While it's tempting to skip this uncomfortable stage to get on with the process of moving forward, the Anger and Bargaining stage serves a useful purpose if used resourcefully – to help us clear out the debris of our collapsed dreams and expectations and make room for the new priorities and values excavated in the following stage of depression, reflection and loneliness.

Cathy's Story

Married for more than 30 years to a professional health care practitioner, Cathy had taken financial security for granted. The bills had always been paid on time. Life was tidy and neat, prosperous and peaceful. Or so she believed. Until it changed.

Her husband walked out of the marriage.

Cathy's entire world was thrown into a financial and emotional tailspin. After the numbness of shock and denial and an intense period of pain and guilt, she turned to anger.

Because her husband had also been her business partner and his practice their sole source of income, she was suddenly adrift. No savings, no paycheck, no retirement fund, IRAs, stock options, investments or insurance. The equity in the family home was dwindling with the falling real estate market and with too many homes on the market the future looked bleak.

She wanted to scream "No Fair! Foul play!" She wanted to bargain with the gods of time and reverse it, go back to the happy family days. The "if only" scenarios ran through her head like a continuous replay. She tried apologizing, pleading, negotiating, threatening and cajoling her former soul mate and lifelong comrade, but to no avail.

Bargaining is another form of denial. It is an attempt to rewrite your reality. It is also a form of procrastination because you end up going nowhere except back to where you started. It buys you time, riding on a merry-go-round of self-rationalization.

Eventually you return to the place where you first refused to acknowledge the reality of the situation. As long as you continue to bargain, you can avoid meeting reality face-to-face, do not have to seek resolution and can delay moving forward.

Get mad, then get over it.
~Colin Powell

Finally, in desperation fueled by her anger and motivated by a zero balance in her bank account, Cathy plunged headlong into survival activity. She started her own practice, offering the same alternative health care services she had offered when in business with her husband.

Eventually, clients followed her, new ones discovered her. It began to seem as though the darkness would make room for a little light, as long as she stayed buried in her work. She was grateful for the productive outlet. Yet, within the social, family and community spheres of her small town, the wound continued to fester. Daily reminders sparked her anger.

It was difficult to concentrate and she exhausted her reserves with the continual effort of trying to avoid painful confrontations or explain herself to concerned friends and clients. She feared her health would suffer and knew she would not heal the hard knot in her heart living this way.

Tired of the daily dose of bitter pills, she began to look for refuge in the idea of moving to another town. It seemed reasonable to allow herself space to heal elsewhere but in these shaky economic times it could be downright foolish to leave a growing business behind. She suffered the classic dilemma of the heart versus the pocketbook. It was a test of her core values.

After months of fretting and vacillating, she chose a compromise. She would move her home to the next town and begin the process of growing yet another new practice. But, unable and unwilling to completely let go of her familiar financial lifeboat, she would continue to commute half the week to her first solo practice.

Out of the frying pan and into the fire, Cathy immediately found herself in dire economic straits. She had to buy a reliable car for the commute and pay higher rent in her new town. Her already small bank account was drained by the second set of startup costs that doubled her business expenses.

She found herself fighting back the financial wolves from her door. Swept up in busyness, commuting long hours from town to town, juggling family time with her children and trying to wrap up the messy details of her former life, her anger and self-doubt simmered, stalling her forward action. Frustrated, she began to worry if she would have to live this split life forever.

> *A clever person turns great troubles into little ones,*
> *and little ones into none at all.*
> ~Chinese Proverb

A coach helped Cathy look at her situation from a new perspective, reconfirm her goals and values and look toward what could be, rather than what was not. She had gotten stuck in her emotions, revving the engine in neutral. With a little help, she drew a clearer picture in her mind of a growing practice in the new town, outlined her goals and listed the steps she needed to take.

With her next actions focused, instead of rolling around and around in her head, her emotions settled down again and she began to take the small, positive steps toward re-establishing her practice and her life in the new town.

"It's easy to get lost in doing non-productive things while you insist on carrying a monstrous emotional burden," she said. "And it doesn't stop the bills from coming in."

Unknowingly, Cathy did what many people do who aren't ready to face the reality of their situation; she mistook the emotional roller coaster of anger and bargaining in her head for action. She spent all her time focusing on inconsequential details rather than the important ones needed to accomplish her goals. Run by her emotions, she lost sight of her priorities. What she couldn't see was that she was expending a lot of energy and effort running in place, treading water and getting nowhere fast.

What works, works. What doesn't work, doesn't work.
And working harder at what doesn't work doesn't make it work.
~Joe Caruso

Fix it Any Way Possible

When we're caught in the Anger and Bargaining stage, we are attempting unsuccessfully to fix our problem by any means possible. The flurry of activity involved in brainstorming, planning and trying to "get something going" feels deceptively good, like we're really doing something to change the situation. Our family and friends are pleased and smile approvingly because they are so happy we've moved beyond the Pain and Guilt stage that made them feel so uncomfortable and helpless.

What isn't clear to us, until it doesn't work, is that when we resort to bargaining with ourselves, spouses, family, bosses or God, it's an attempt to deny and shield us from the pain, a natural part of the healing process. Ultimately, it won't resolve anything or move us forward where we truly want to go. And when our well-meaning efforts only offset our loss, we eventually collapse and plunge into the despair we were desperate to avoid.

Bargaining can take other forms, often appearing as common sense. We roll over the balance from one credit card to another, ostensibly to save money with a lower interest rate. We launch into buying household items or clothing on sale or in bulk to save money in the long run. We gravitate to one get-rich scheme after another, thinking "if only I can…" We're ready and willing to bargain with anyone or anything we perceive as having the ability to influence our predicament. And we're more willing to take risks we would otherwise never consider.

Bargaining Turns to Anger

When the bargaining house of cards falls apart – and it will – our frustration at this additional loss turns to anger at ourselves, our spouse, our family, the unfairness of the situation. The list is endless. We can get caught in an endless cycle of consuming self-blame and self-recrimination as the tape of what we "woulda, coulda and shoulda done" replays over and over in our minds.

Anger is one letter short of danger.
~Eleanor Roosevelt

A sense of justification and entitlement to our anger rears up and we may lash out without thinking, hurting feelings and damaging relationships. The unintended consequences of inappropriately venting our anger will further cloud our judgment and unhinge our emotions, creating a vicious spiral of anger, blame and fear.

To be clear, this anger is not to be repressed or denied. It will boil over and cause hurt to others and ourselves if not released. Denied anger can lead to serious health problems including heart disease, emotional and mental distress, sleep disorders, liver issues, indigestion and bowel problems. Burying the anger doesn't resolve the underlying problem and can undermine our closest relationships.

Anger, like fear, might best be viewed as a red flag signaling there is something beneath the surface that needs urgent investigation. Anger is typically labeled as a "bad" or "negative" emotion, but anger can be a very productive emotion. It's showing us where to dig for the truth. It can clear internal landfills of repressed and denied emotions out of the way so more authentic and healthy relationships with others and ourselves can begin to grow.

Expressing Anger Productively

The trick to using anger productively is expressing it with awareness of how you are affected without blaming yourself or others, no small feat. Otherwise, anger can easily be misinterpreted as criticism and blame. For example, a couple that becomes fearful about the diminishing balance in their checking account may express that as anger at the other partner's purchases. Then each partner becomes offended and angry and the underlying fear and problem has no chance of being addressed.

It's common for people to misdirect anger outside of themselves. As in the bargaining part of this stage, it feels safe to redirect that anger at the government, corporate America, outmoded and inefficient systems in our workplace, unproductive colleagues, credit card companies, mortgage companies – there are many potential candidates we feel are worthy of our anger. While none on this list is blameless, keeping the focus of our anger *on others* only serves to distract us from dealing with our role in our anger.

While in anger it is important to understand it is also part of the healing process of grief and a stage to steer through with tenderness. You may have every right to feel angry but you don't have the right to destructively vent that anger on others. Prolonging the time you spend in anger will only cause you harm and stall the healing process.

Anger ventilated often hurries toward forgiveness;
and concealed often hardens into revenge.
~Edward G. Bulwer-Lytton

Insights

Anger is a rocky sea through which a navigator searches for calmer water.

- Understand that anger cannot be denied or ignored. If you find yourself countering responses to your anger with, "Yeah, but..." you may want to look at whether you are willing to own your anger (without blame) and your part in it.
- Anger is often nature's way of holding up a mirror. People, situations or events that make us angry often reflect back something about ourselves we don't like. What can you notice about your anger that feels familiar?

- Recognize that anger is fear turned outward. It's a red flag showing us where to look deeper. What's under your anger? Perhaps fear and insecurity about an unknown future?

Exercises

Observe, acknowledge and release anger

1. Set aside a few hours and take a short drive to a place where you can be alone and surrounded by nature. Bring along paper and pencil or a journal. Find a comfortable spot to sit and try saying "hello" to your anger. Approach your anger as if it were a stranger and foreign to you.

    Then try to simply watch your angry thoughts from a neutral place without projecting them onto someone or something else. Experiment with engaging all of your senses to get to know your angry thoughts. What do they look like, feel like, smell like, sound like? What do they have to teach you? Write down your observations. Stay in this observing mode as long as you need to learn about your anger. It may take time to get beyond the natural resistance.

2. What are some of the things you are angry at that relate to your present financial situation? What are the fears under that anger? Write down your observations.

3. You may want to consider writing down your anger observations in a private journal. If keeping a private

journal feels too risky in case someone might find it, you may consider writing these observations on loose sheets of paper and burning the pages or tearing them into hundreds of tiny pieces, a safe physical and symbolic way to express and release that anger at the end of your brief nature retreat.

4. Is there someone you trust to whom you can express your anger without repercussions? Contact that person and ask if he or she is willing to be a sounding board, listening without judgment, comment or trying to "fix" your anger or situation.

5. If you feel uncomfortable expressing your anger to a friend or loved one, consider seeing a professional who is trained to listen and find the gold under your anger. Or visit www.LemonadeNetwork.com to find a helpful and compassionate coach to fit your needs.

6. Many people use physical exercise as a healthy way of burning off anger without hurting themselves or anyone else. Daily walks are a healthy way to help you release anger as you get in touch with the feelings and fears under the anger.

Moving On

Once you run out of anger as fuel, which can make you sick, lose friends as well as say and do things you'll regret later, you're ready to move into what can be an unexpectedly valuable stage of grief – Depression, Reflection and Loneliness.

CHAPTER 5

Stage 4: Depression, Reflection, Loneliness

Depression, reflection and loneliness often follow anger and bargaining. As you reflect on the magnitude of your situation, it is normal to feel stuck, overwhelmed, discouraged and isolated. By observing your feelings and behavior patterns and considering new ways of thinking and reacting, you'll gain insights into how to put this stage behind you.

You may be asking yourself what could be "unexpectedly valuable" about going through depression, reflection and loneliness. You'd think that if you survived the pain, guilt, anger and bargaining, that would be enough, right?

These stages are difficult and trying. The emotional toll can result in a desire to retreat, a fear of not being able to overcome, a physical exhaustion.

Stay with us. Read on and we will show you why this next stage is so valuable and necessary to your journey.

When it is dark enough, you can see the stars.
~Ralph Waldo Emerson

Jerry's Story

Jerry awakened with a start and looked at the clock. Why didn't the alarm go off? It was almost 6:30 a.m. and he was supposed to be at work at 7a.m.! He was never late for work. He threw back the covers and started to jump out of bed.

"Wait a minute. Don't you remember what happened yesterday?" his half-awake subconscious shouted. With a groan that sounded almost like a sob, he lay back down as the memory flooded his mind.

It had been a typical Monday morning, just one of almost 2,000 Mondays he had spent at the same company. Only this Monday morning rocked his world.

About mid-morning, he was called to his manager's office. That was not unusual. He was often called in to discuss quality control or safety issues in the company, asked his opinion or given a special project.

But this meeting was not the usual. He knew as soon as he looked at his manager's face when he walked into the office that it was not good news. But his mind still couldn't imagine the bomb that was about to drop.

"Jerry, we're going to have to lay you off. We've been given a directive to cut staff and payroll so we're going to have to let you go. I'll go with you to get your personal things and walk you to the door."

WHAT? He thought he must have been hearing things. Why would a company lay off an employee of almost 39 years? One who could do almost any job in the company? Surely they could find another position for him!

But it was very clear that his manager was serious.

The thing that made no sense to Jerry was why his manager felt the need to escort him to pick up his things and did not want to give him a chance to say goodbye to his long-time friends and co-workers. That probably hurt and bewildered him more than anything.

Fast-forward Six Months

The television was on a woodworking show he always enjoyed, but Jerry found himself staring at the floor, his mind a blur. He was still not sleeping well at night and was spending way too much time just sitting and staring, living on memories, playing the "what if" game and feeling like the world had moved on and left him sitting still.

Why was he not getting responses to more than 200 resumes he had sent out? He made sure to send them to companies that should welcome a person with his years of experience in design and manufacturing of precision equipment and tools. So why? He knew that few people have such a broad range of expertise in these areas, so why couldn't these companies see what his skills and experience could do for them?

It must be because he was 57 years old and they're looking for fresh, young talent with a college degree in engineering, not someone who's ready to be "put out to pasture."

Jerry had always been so proud of being responsible and always providing for his family. Now he couldn't even get a response to a single resume. What was he going to do? He felt totally worthless, a burden on his wife, who had suddenly become the sole support for their household.

The Struggles

It was all he could do to be around well-meaning friends who wanted to pull him out of his desire to be alone. He didn't feel like laughing and joking like he had always done. Why couldn't they leave him alone? He remembered a quote he once saw from Olin Miller: *"What a pity human beings can't exchange problems. Everyone knows exactly how to solve the other fellow's."* His friends had no idea what this felt like. And laughing and joking didn't make it go away.

Even though he loved his family with a passion, especially his grandchildren, it was very hard to laugh and play with them. And of course, they didn't understand why grandpa was so cranky.

Jerry had always been a creature of habit. He was used to waking up at 6 a.m., driving the same route to work, working diligently, playing dominoes at lunch in the break room, taking the same route home, eating at the same time every evening, going to bed at the same time.

Boy, was he messed up now! He still wanted to get up at 6 a.m., but he wasn't sleeping well. He couldn't seem to turn his mind off at night. And when he finally did fall asleep, the bad dreams wouldn't stop. If he did get up at 6 a.m., it made the day longer while he waited for the phone to ring or the mail to be delivered.

Silly as it may seem, one of the things he missed most was the lunchtime domino game in the company break room. He and his coworkers had done it for years. Now, he wasn't even hungry at lunchtime.

Depression

One of the classic effects of this stage of the grieving process is a deep feeling of depression, a feeling that nothing positive, nothing joyful, nothing promising will ever cross your path again.

Calls to the National Suicide Prevention hotline are up a staggering 50 percent this year, a frightening statistic. It is sobering to think of the additional number of people who have not had the courage to call but who may be in a very deep depression, wondering if there will ever be a way out.

Can you hear the depression in Jerry's story? The sounds of helplessness, hopelessness, and overwhelming feeling of despair. "How dare they toss me aside – out with the day's trash?" His American Dream was not for wealth or fame, but just to contribute his talents and knowledge to advance his company's success and retire comfortably when the time came. But even this simple American Dream died an untimely death.

Reflection

Another classic effect of this stage of grief can almost be classified as an obsession. The griever *constantly* reflects on the situation and what caused his current crisis. He may spend hours reliving in his mind the shock, anger and fear that preceded his current depression.

Can you feel Jerry's pain as he reflects on the injustice and the impersonal way he was dismissed without warning? The way he is trying to figure out how to deal with the impact? You can hear these thoughts running through his head:

- "My small unemployment check is running out and I'm getting scared."
- "Why didn't I save more money all these years?"
- "Why didn't I concentrate on paying off the house?"
- "Why did we take that vacation?"
- "I promised my wife if she'd quit her corporate job, I'd take care of all the household expenses."

You can clutch the past so tightly to your chest that it leaves your
arms too full to embrace the present.
~Jan Glidewell

Loneliness

The third classic effect of this stage of grief is a feeling of isolation, of being totally alone to deal with the death of your American Dream. Yes, friends and family offer their support and want to give you advice, but you've never felt so alone in your life. Even in a room full of people, you can feel total separation from everyone, isolated in your own bubble, left to find your own way to survive.

In Jerry's case, being suddenly cut off from the friends he had cultivated for years was, indeed, like the sudden unexpected loss of a loved one. It was like what you would experience if a friend or loved one had an accident and you couldn't be with them as you normally would.

"How can I possibly be lonely with a wife, kids, grandkids, church, friends and neighbors who love me and are so concerned about helping me move forward?" Jerry often asked himself.

They Just Don't Understand

In Jerry's case, he was feeling the full blow of the loss of a huge part of his identity. When you have diligently given every working day of your adult life to one company, it feels like a hole has been punched in your spirit, like a huge balloon stabbed with a knife.

Over and over, he kept asking himself, "What am I going to do? Who am I now?"

His friends thought he should force himself to be happy and sociable, that he should move on and forget about what had happened. If they had any idea how hard it was just to get up in the morning and get dressed, they would back off. He needed some space to work through things. He didn't need this added pressure! No wonder he wanted to be alone so much of the time.

Getting Out of This Funk

This fourth in the stages of grief is another necessary stage to go through. That's the key...to go *through* it and not remain here at length.

There is no correct amount of time to spend in this stage. Each individual works through it at his own pace. It is healthy and helpful to have supportive, loving family and friends, but working through grief is a very personal task.

Don't be surprised if you occasionally seem to revisit a prior stage in the grieving process. It happened to Jerry and it may happen from time to time as you work your way along this path.

"For the most part, I've gotten through the daily pain and guilt, but they still creep back in, just when I think I'm making progress," Jerry confided. "Yes, I've gotten through the anger (most of the time) and when I catch myself bargaining, it's with God: 'If you'll just please help me find a job, I swear I'll never again complain about the petty things regarding my job or my salary or upper management.'"

As Jerry worked through the stages of the death of his American Dream, he became aware of the potential that lay in turning his hobby into a profession. He had always enjoyed woodworking, building cabinets, rebuilding and remodeling and general household repair. Opening his own business as a handyman seemed the logical choice for getting out of his dilemma. As he developed this business, he experienced a great deal of satisfaction and was rewarded by the expressions of appreciation from his customers.

Effect on Health

The sorrow which has no vent in tears may make
other organs weep.
~Henry Maudsley

Among the numerous effects on a person's health, conditions such as teeth grinding, fatigue, anxiety, insomnia, headaches, depression, stress-induced ulcers, panic attacks, increased smoking or drinking, detachment, withdrawal from social interaction, irritability and brain fog can often be traced to grief.

If the depression stage is allowed to continue for an extended period of time, more serious health conditions can result such as hypertension, diabetes, weight issues, bowel problems, rashes and others. Be keenly aware of your feelings as you work through this stage. Realize that if your depression becomes deep and life threatening, or just more than you can handle, please don't continue to ignore it. A licensed healthcare professional should be consulted to evaluate and address it.

Being vs. Doing

All your adult life, you've been constantly busy, always "doing." These new circumstances have turned your routine upside down. Now, you find yourself more in the state of "being" while trying to find the energy and ambition to get back to "doing."

The state of "being" can be a very healthy and beneficial state, if used properly. It can result in an in-depth search of a person's values, goals and desires. However, if used incorrectly, it can result in drifting through the days without making an effort to change your current state.

Questions

Following are some questions to ask yourself as you assess where you are in the journey and some statements that may be made by a person in the Depression, Reflection, Loneliness stage:

- No, I can't come to the family picnic. I'm not feeling well.
- I really miss those co-workers who had become such good friends over the years.
- Maybe if I'd tried harder to get management to see where we needed to make some changes, the company could have been more profitable.
- They were right. I'm a loser. There's no point in trying to get another job – no one would hire me.
- Are you at a loss for what to do with yourself?
- Are you sleeping during the day?
- Do you find yourself eating or drinking to excess to numb the pain?
- Are your emotions out of control?
- Do you find yourself too easily irritated?
- Do you find yourself "kicking the cat" or taking your anger out on those closest to you?
- Do you find yourself staring mindlessly at the TV hour after hour, with little motivation to get moving?
- Do you keep yourself occupied with meaningless busy tasks?
- Do you avoid returning phone calls, responding to email or setting up dates with friends?

If you answered, "Yes" to several of these questions or can relate to some of the statements, you are probably experiencing the Depression, Reflection, Loneliness stage of the grieving process.

Insights

Within this chapter's journey through the Depression, Reflection, Loneliness stage of grief, we have discussed several key factors to helping you move forward through this stage. Let's summarize a couple of them.

- Regardless of the magnitude of your American Dream, the loss is just as devastating to you as someone whose dream is much larger. Jerry's dream wasn't lofty according to the world's standards, but losing it turned his world upside down. However, by acknowledging his loss and deciding not to remain in his funk, he turned it around. Jerry made the choice to pick up the pieces and move on and, as a result, he created a new dream.

- Ignoring it, pushing it down, hiding from it doesn't make it go away. The saying "Time heals all wounds" is only true if we choose to change our outlook and/or our circumstances. Had Jerry chosen to remain isolated and living in the past, he would have never embarked on his new career. He would have remained in depression, reflection and loneliness for years. He would have missed the challenge and satisfaction he now enjoys with his new business and the restored connections with his family and friends.

Exercises

1. Take a serious, non-judgmental look at the way you've been feeling and responding. Try to measure it. On a scale of 1 to 10, with '1' being 'in total darkness with no hope at all' and '10' being 'heaven on earth', how would you rate your current state of depression?
    Your rating (1-10) _____ Does that surprise you? Are you happy with your rating?

2.   Whenever you find yourself feeling depressed or lonely, try slow, methodical deep breathing. Try this: Sit up very straight, pull your shoulders back and tummy in, hold your chin up and breathe in slowly, counting to ten. Hold that breath for 10 counts, then exhale slowly to the count of 10. Repeat six times while thinking of a place or an event when you were happy and involved with life.

3. Recognize that physical activity is very important to both your body and your mind. You don't have to go to the gym for a workout. Try walking up and down the stairs a few times or walking around your neighborhood or the mall or bouncing on your kids' trampoline to get yourself moving. Any of those mild activities will help. Be creative. Find simple ways that will get you up and moving, get your heart rate up a little bit, and get you out of the house and breathing a little deeper. You'll be surprised how much this will help improve your mood.

4. Write in a Gratitude Journal every night. Think of at least one thing for which you are grateful. When you're feeling down, go back and look at entries you've made. It will lift your spirits and make it easier for you to think more positive thoughts.

Birds sing after a storm; why shouldn't people feel as free to delight in whatever remains to them?
~Rose F. Kennedy

Moving On

Like every stage discussed in the book, moving forward through this stage is a choice. It is a conscious decision to move out of the feelings of depression, reflection and loneliness into an upward turn.

There are helpful resources in this book as well as many tools and events on www.LemonadeNetwork.com. Let us know how we can help you.

The next chapter will guide you into that positive change, that upward turn you've been yearning for. Don't stop now! You're on the verge of making some powerful changes to your life.

The secret to getting ahead is getting started.
~Mark Twain

CHAPTER 6

Stage 5: The Upward Turn

The Upward Turn is a vulnerable and fragile time, as we turn and begin to climb out of the depths of pain, denial, anger and depression, accepting what was while focusing on the future with a new perspective.

The sense of relief and exhilaration in the Upward Turn can deceive us into thinking and feeling that we've arrived at the end of this painful trek. While we will feel a flush of new energy at leaving the pain behind, it is also a vulnerable time as we step out of depression, reflection and loneliness and embark on a new road with an uncertain destination. The key to successfully crossing this stage is movement and action despite uncertainty.

Marsha's Story

It was late morning of Sept. 3, 2008, and Marsha was watching a stock option trade she had just entered. The stock market had opened up that day and because this stock chart had all the indications it could be a nice little trade, she felt pretty confident about making a profit on this one.

Then some bad news hit and the market, as it was prone during this volatile period, started to act like an out-of-control roller coaster. In less than 30 minutes, Marsha watched the profits she had eked out over the last month vanish as she scrambled to exit the trade while the stock kept plummeting, along with the Dow and NASDAQ.

After she was finally out of the trade, her account nearly $500 lighter, she logged out of her brokerage account, shut down the computer and pushed away from the desk shouting to no one, "Enough! That's it! I'm done!" The tension Marsha had carried for three years burst like a popped balloon.

As option trades go, it was a not a large trade. But neither was Marsha's trading account at that point, after losing nearly three-quarters of it in July 2008 during one of the market's freaky headlong dips. She had six trades open then, and froze like a deer in the headlights, watching as the losses mounted. She couldn't believe she was doing what she swore she would never do – break the trading rules she had been taught to watch herself go down in flames.

Marsha quit trading cold turkey, staying away from her online brokerage account to check stock charts or read market news. This was a radical change for a woman who was determined to make a living with her brains and guts by trading. She had spent eight to 10 hours per day for a couple of years studying stock charts, along with thousands of dollars and countless additional hours reading, studying and learning with a trading coach.

She flew to workshops in Salt Lake City and Atlanta. She bought a laptop computer to be her office away from home. She checked charts and trades at night in hotel rooms when she traveled. Marsha traded tips and offered advice to "newbies" in trading chat rooms. She made friends through trading. And then she simply turned it off and headed in another direction.

This is one version of the upward turn. You could call it the "aha" moment, one of those startling moments of clarity often portrayed in the movies. Our heroine finally gets it. She realized that what she has been doggedly pursuing against all odds was not working and she pulled up stakes. She looked around with new eyes and saw the mess her life had become in the absence of her presence. She turned and courageously moved in a new direction, her head held high.

Marsha looked around for immediate opportunities to generate cash, swallowed her pride and began cleaning houses.

As is often the case, the beginning of Marsha's upward turn wasn't glorious or romantic. There was no clever photography or dramatic movie soundtracks. There was only her strangled yelp in a silent house as the heavy weight of the truth hit her. She had been bargaining with time and now she held the losing hand. Then her stomach rolled over. Freed from the chains of the computer and watching stock charts all day, Marsha experienced a surge of energy she hadn't felt in the three years since she lost her job and with money in the bank, began a self-declared sabbatical to discover new paths. Now, terrified she would run out of money, Marsha flew into frantic, frenetic action. She began searching for jobs online, networking through email, setting up meetings and lining up housecleaning clients to bring in some cash.

Marsha had always found housecleaning easy and somewhat satisfying, so she was shocked at how long it took her to do even the simplest tasks and how difficult it was to estimate her time on a job. Her underlying guilt over the financial mess she had created was compounded by the inadequacy she felt at being unable to streamline the work and pick up speed. Exhausted and sore after 10 hours hauling a vacuum up and down stairs cleaning up after heavily shedding dogs, Marsha gained an unexpected new respect for people who cleaned for a living.

She lost weight during those two months and got into better shape, but she could never shut off her calculating brain that mercilessly reminding her she was not earning enough and "things" weren't happening quickly enough to allow her to survive financially.

Housecleaning, which is ripe with metaphors for change and renewal, gave Marsha time to think and ponder. Even as she pushed down the fear that crept up and grabbed her stomach regularly and kept her awake at night, she also became aware of several new undercurrents of energy coursing through her life.

Awareness Expands Vision

The piercing awareness that cut through Marsha's internal wall of denial that ordinary day had expanded into a horizon-to-horizon awareness of how life and the world had moved on while she was actually treading water but pretending she was swimming with the current. She realized how disconnected she was from the energy of life. This is one of the cues that the upward turn has taken hold.

Gathering her daily news selectively online and communicating through email and in chat rooms had isolated Marsha in a self-built silo, where she could only see what her tiny windows on the world allowed her to see. Now she had the full and disturbing view of how her life had continued on its downward spiral while she bargained with the market: "If I can only make $100 a day…$75 a day…$50 a day…"

She tried to refrain from self-blame, but the inner voice persisted. "You woulda...You coulda...You shoulda..."

Urgency Shifts into High Gear

Marsha needed to find something that worked and she needed to find it immediately. Any prior pickiness over what kind of work she would accept disappeared along with the money in her bank account. Nothing happened quickly enough, even as she tried to remember that her worries were not a priority for others, for they had their own. After being stuck in self-reflection for so long, an overpowering sense of urgency is a signal of movement into the upward turn.

Energy Released

Freed from the tight box of denial and self-reflection she had built and fueled by the urgency of her situation, Marsha's energy soared and stayed high. Not only did she clean other people's houses, she cleaned her own – physically, emotionally, mentally and energetically. Every day as she moved forward step-by-step she was able to look back and see how far behind she had fallen into isolation and denial. This is a clear sign that the trance of the Depression stage is broken – high energy and the impulse to change.

More Calm, Less Chaos

After the initial explosive surge of blocked energy, a quiet sense of calm snuck up on Marsha. She experienced fewer mood swings and anxiety attacks. The physical symptoms of anxiety lessened – the constantly churning stomach, sleeplessness, worry, anxiousness and muscular tension in her neck and shoulders.

Marsha took comfort and hope in the fact that she had a plan and was taking action on that plan. On more days than not, she felt a sense of balance and equilibrium begin to offset the anxiety and worry. It wasn't perfect but she was moving. Having a plan and acting on it – even though you're still unsure of the outcome – is a sign the upward turn is in motion.

Allowing Space for the Present

As she shifted her focus from the death grip she had on what was not working to allowing space for new possibilities, Marsha was able to think beyond her current struggles for the first time. And ironically, that began with a firm grounding in the present with a verbal slap upside the head from a business coach.

After listening to Marsha's anxiety-laced tale of woe for a few minutes the coach interrupted in a quiet but insistent voice.

"What if there is nothing to get through, Marsha? What if this is it? What if this is all there is?"

Another "aha" moment: Was life really so bad? Or was it her attitude about her life that needed changing? What was the worst that could happen? Where did the change need to begin?

Vulnerable and Fragile

The Upward Turn is a vulnerable and fragile time. While we have turned and begun a climb out of the depths of pain, denial, anger and depression, our footing isn't sure and secure yet. Slipping back a step or two periodically and repeatedly is easy and common. It's going to happen, so expect it.

This stage is often characterized by polarities because our heightened awareness has opened to allow us to see – and hold – two opposites simultaneously but without the intense pain we've previously experienced. Still, we may not be sure which way to go.

So while we have a sense of urgency to move forward quickly, it is tempered by a new inner knowing that we can't take on too much too quickly. We begin to consider and plan for change and we're able to pace ourselves sensibly.

The Upward Turn is being able to hold two different experiences and emotions simultaneously: sadness over the past and glimmerings of hope for the future.

It's also two opposite actions at the same time: Beginning to walk away from what was and toward what will be. It's the beginning of acceptance of the way things are now while focusing on future plans.

It's realizing you need to take the next step without knowing exactly where the path will take you or what is around the corner. Then taking the next step, and the next.

The Upward Turn can be compared to the classic hills and valleys on stock charts. After hitting the proverbial "bottom," a stock often stays at the bottom of the valley for some time while moving up and down in a tight pattern. Experienced traders refer to this pattern as consolidation or building a base. Once a stock has built a solid enough base, only then has it amassed the energy to sustain an uphill climb.

People moving through the stages of grief behave in the same way. Only when we've stayed in the valley of depression, reflection and loneliness long enough have we consolidated enough energy to sustain an upward turn. Still, we will be tested during this vulnerable and fragile time, often slipping back a few steps and having to start the climb again.

The Air Gets Clearer as You Climb

You can now see the value of the previous stages of grief, as you gain a calmer perspective during the Upward Turn. This awareness of how you got to where you are, without the previous pain and self-judgment, creates space for new thoughts of a new future to emerge.

We experience an exhilarating sense of freedom and anticipation knowing we're starting to climb out of the pain, denial and depression into fresher air while we're fully cognizant there will be work ahead.

One of the most important things to learn about the Upward Turn is that we can choose something fresh. The Upward Turn is not another chance to work harder at what didn't work but to use these valuable stages of self-reflection to re-examine and recommit to our deepest values and passions.

Once we get clear of pain, denial and depression, we get the opportunity to look for answers to the "What if..." questions we've buried. Marsha, who was hell-bent on achieving financial independence on her own terms, got to grapple with the question "What if I have to take a job to stabilize my situation? Will I never become financially independent?"

It never occurred to her that she might gain valuable skills, contacts and resources that could aid her entrepreneurial ambitions. She also never realized that the self-discipline she gained while trading would give her more inner resources to rely on to continue building a business on her own time while also being successful at a job.

The new awareness we gain during the Upward Turn gives us a wonderful chance to reframe our circumstances without self-blame and self-recrimination, if we allow it to happen. The Upward Turn is a pivotal moment between the painful past and the unknown future. It allows us to move forward and upward without dragging along the baggage and debris of the past while still making the most of the lessons we've learned.

In Your Own Time

There's an inherent and organic wisdom in letting the Upward Turn come at its own pace, as we allow ourselves to fully process the grief and pain and start to heal as we reflect. It's unlikely we'll start the Upward Turn fast enough for most of our friends and family, who are experiencing extreme discomfort watching us grieve and wanting us to feel better so they can feel better about their own lives. It's a challenge to not move ahead until we're ready, if moving ahead really means soothing other people's fears.

The Upward Turn is only reached when we can finally settle in the neutral center between the two polarities of our experience, the calm middle ground between despair and joy. This is that peaceful place inside of us that is without fear, without doubt, without judgment, without worry. From here we have the freedom to move in any direction we desire. We can't always explain it, but we know it's right.

While most people are paralyzed by the unknown consequences of changing, it is important to be clear about the consequences of not changing, of staying stuck. In this instance, Marsha would have lost the benefit of using the balance of her account to stop this accelerating downward financial spiral. In hindsight, she realized the chances were good she would have continued to lose money, would have had to borrow money to live on and likely filed for bankruptcy. The anxiety and worry would have continued to mount and she would have felt tremendous self-blame and self-judgment for the financial mess she had created with little financial or emotional relief in sight.

Cues You are Now in the Upward Turn

- When you start to feel frustrated with what you've been feeling and what you've been through, you're on your way into the Upward Turn.
- When staying where you are starts to feel uncomfortable and your thoughts start to wander toward the future – and stay there – you're on your way into the Upward Turn.
- When doing that doesn't feel like turning your back on the life that was, you're firmly in the Upward Turn.

Upward Turn Thoughts and Questions

- You know, I'll really miss this house. But maybe it will be much less stressful to start over in a smaller house and simpler lifestyle.
- It's up to me to get on with my life. Nobody else is going to do it for me.
- The world didn't end when my retirement plans were crushed. The sun still comes up, the birds still sing. My kids/grandkids still love me and that's what is most important.
- I'm still just as smart and capable and hardworking as I was before.
- What else would I like to do?

- What would make me happy? What would be fun, for a change?

What do happiness and fun look like, feel like, taste like and smell like now?

- If I have my choice, how would I like to earn my income and spend my time now?

> *Two of the greatest and saddest words*
> *in the English language are, What if...*
> ~Joe Caruso

Insights

If you are to progress through this stage you need to get clear on what needs to change:

- Understand what is no longer working and stop doing it. Marsha could have continued to try to generate income by trading small positions that would only continue to give her a pittance for her time and expense, while she kept desperately hoping for some home runs in a market challenging even for seasoned traders.
- Give yourself permission to move in a new direction and don't agonize over finding the perfect next step. Perfection isn't necessary or needed. Movement is. Take action, however small. And then celebrate the decision!

Marsha wasn't thrilled about cleaning houses, but she was grateful for the opportunity to earn cash on her own terms. When a full-time job presented itself when she didn't expect it, she found a professional housecleaner who had just lost clients and who was thrilled to take Marsha's clients.

- Accept that you'll make mistakes and there will be missteps. Failure isn't in making mistakes; it's in stopping and refusing to learn from your mistakes. Keep going, even though you don't know exactly what lies ahead or what you will find.

The moment one definitely commits oneself, then providence moves too. A whole stream of events issue from the decision, raising in one's favor all manner of unforeseen incidents, meetings and material assistance, which no man could have dreamt would have come his way.

~W.H. Murray, The Scottish Himalayan Expedition, 1951

Exercises

Set aside an hour when you can be undisturbed. Now that your head is clearing the clouds of depression, take a look at where you are, where you need to be and where you want to go.

1. Label four clean sheets of paper with these titles:
    a) Two Weeks
    b) One Month
    c) Two Months
    d) Three Months

2. On the paper titled **Two Weeks** quickly write all the things you will need to do in the next two weeks to move you ahead one step on your plan. List the calls you've avoided making while you were in the Depression, Self-Reflection and Loneliness stage. Include the resumes and letters you've been meaning to mail and any other small steps that you can accomplish quickly and feel good knowing you are doing what you can do in the moment.
    Marsha called potential cleaning clients until she made contact and quickly made appointments to meet them. She reactivated her network, calling the most likely contacts that might know of or have jobs available. At night, she scanned the job boards.

3. Consider where you want to be in one month, two months and three months. Begin jotting down small steps you'll need to take to help you get there, whether it's as simple as a phone call, making a date for lunch or tackling a pile of paperwork so you can hunt for information on starting a business or going back to school. Cut down the tasks into small steps and give yourself reasonable, achievable goals over the next two months.

4. Write down the steps on the appropriate paper. Don't worry about where you'll be in a month or two or how you'll get it done. Write down the tasks and dates on a calendar or in a planner.

5. Aim to keep yourself moving. You've gotten this far through the stages of grief; give yourself permission to

trust that the process will take you there. If you need help and don't feel you can do it alone, contact The Lemonade Network and we'll discuss what we can do to help.

Start by doing what's necessary; then do what's possible;
and suddenly you are doing the impossible.
~Francis of Assisi

Moving On

Whichever direction you decide to head as you enter The Upward Turn, this is the point where you get to choose: Will you move forward, or will you stay stuck? The Upward Turn is not about taking huge, risk-filled actions and grandiose plans. It's about taking advantage of the time we've had to be still and reflective and making progressive, small steps in the direction we want to go. As we do that, we build momentum and energy that can be sustained for the next phase of this process, the Reconstruction and Working Through stage.

If you think you could use some help navigating the Upward Turn, a Lemonade Network coach can help you explore and reframe the possibilities while you keep moving forward on your path. Visit www.LemonadeNetwork.com and click "Contact us" or take a look at the available programs.

You've made it through the toughest and most painful stages. While the rest of the journey won't be easy, it will be easier and you can begin to take deeper breaths as you become more aware that you've made the turn and are on your way again. Bravo!

Whatever you can do or dream you can, begin it.
Boldness has genius, power, and magic in it.
~Johann Wolfgang von Goethe

CHAPTER 7

Stage 6: Reconstruction and Working Through

> **The reconstruction stage** gives you the opportunity to redefine your situation and reconnect with your inner assets to set a direction for additional action. You add more tools to rebuild your dream.

Re-creation. Let's break the word down...Re-create:
To create again, begin again, to start over...Re-creation isn't about relaxing. It is about redefining...whatever's become undefined.
~Joan of Arcadia episode

In this sixth stage, we can now build on the momentum of the upward turn to move beyond the initial action steps and emerge from survival toward "thrival." How? By taking some time to redefine ourselves and let go of our "story," we create new choices and regain a sense of control. As a result, we feel more confident and we increase the actions to move us toward what we want.

Andrea's Story

"I'm tired of being in survival mode!" Andrea had sobbed to her friend not so long ago. "I want a life! I want to be financially stable *and* I want to be able to retire someday before I die!" Tammy listened with patience and compassion. She'd stood by Andrea as her financial stability, life and self-esteem had unraveled.

A year before, Andrea had been a single woman of 47 without a job. She had been advised to file for bankruptcy. She had mounting debt from graduate school and half her retirement had disappeared. As is the case with most of the stories in this book, she had started out in shock and denial. Her brother's persistence and kindness, for which she was so grateful, helped her move past the shock and denial stage and get on a different track.

Still, the future had seemed bleak and out of Andrea's control. She had cycled in and out of the various initial stages for the better part of that year. Fear had gripped her very core as she imagined the worst possible outcomes. She was consumed with "what ifs" that had let her imagination run wild. Sleep had eluded her and stress enveloped her. She had blamed herself, the world. Andrea had been angry with herself and everyone else, but now she was starting to feel better.

As she wove her way between stages, working through the pain and guilt and learning how to release the anger and self-doubt had been a series of intense challenges. She had acquired some great tools and insights in the process. As hard as it was to ask for and accept help, Andrea realized that the support of her family, friends and colleagues had given her a sense of constancy that allowed her to grow and dig out of the depression and isolation. Her yoga practice and set of flash cards with gratitude statements, prayers and positive affirmations helped her focus on a daily basis and process these stages.

Andrea had been heartened by the "aha" of the upward turn a few months before her conversation with Tammy and, with her brother's help, had taken initial steps to stabilize her situation. So, Andrea had a glimmer of hope that she could get past her circumstances. She knew that, at one level, she had created this and was aware of the problems. She also knew, at another level, she was the one who had to dig herself out. She was tired of living in the past, living in her "story." Now Andrea wanted more concrete, longer-term strategies to re-create her future. What wasn't entirely clear was what, how or where to start.

"Something needs to change," Tammy said. "You're clearly frustrated, unhappy and in pain. You have gathered all kinds of data. You have made a few steps forward but you need to take more definitive action. You need to continue, every day, just taking one little step toward a better future."

Andrea knew she was right. After her sobs subsided and she settled down, Tammy spoke. "So, you want something different than what you have now. You have the opportunity to do it. What do you want? What do think will help you get that? How do you plan to go about getting what you want?"

There comes a point as we work through the stages of grief we know we need to take more definite action, to work through emotions and obstacles and rebuild. But how might you know when it is time to move on and start to re-create? Here are some clues.

Most of the time Andrea had been feeling like something had to change. Are you feeling restless with the way things currently are and longing for something different? In other words, is the pain of staying where you are greater than concerns about what may lie ahead?

Are you tired of telling your "story" and find that it is distracting you from moving forward? Andrea realized as she recounted her story to friends and relatives it was getting old for them and for her. As the story grew cold, she started to dream a bit about possible options, positive "what ifs" if she *were* to take a few steps in a different direction. With time, the pros of moving on and creating a new future became more important than staying stuck in pity and the same circumstances.

If, like Andrea, you find that your story is getting tiresome and the pain of staying where you are is greater than the anxiety of taking steps into a new future, it may be time to re-create a new future. If your thoughts about finding a new direction and new lease on life are becoming more frequent and you see you have new options with new potential that are much more attractive than what you currently have, it may be time for re-creation.

Are you considering making some changes in the next six months? These feelings and clues suggest that you are in the Reconstruction and Working Through stage of the grieving process.

Define What has Become Undefined

The things we encounter in stage six of this model of grief are similar to what one experiences in remodeling a home. For both, we need to start with some basic ideas. Both require a vision of what needs to be different and a basic concept of what it will be like when completed. Both require we consider what things are truly valuable and how high they rank on the priority list.

First, we need a vision of what it is we want. When Tammy asked, "What do you want?" Andrea really didn't have an answer. She realized that she was no longer sure who she was or what she wanted. She had once held a tenured faculty position at a university at the top of her profession. Her self-worth and identity had been tied up in her professional work and academic title. When the "evil dean from hell" insisted that she go back to graduate school, it was the beginning of the end of this professional life. (In retrospect, it was the best thing that could have happened.) It precipitated a career change. This, plus a failed business, a poor investment decision and other financial setbacks had taken Andrea from a respected, sought-after university faculty member to a graduate student with lots of debt trying to subsist on research assistant wages.

Re-creation is about "redefining whatever's become undefined." In one sense, Andrea had become undefined, partly because her definition was based on what had been a successful career and prestigious position, perceptions of what others and society may value. Her self-esteem, which wasn't great to start, was at an all-time low.

If we want to remodel a room, we know that the value of that room has more to do with its basic structure, function and integrity of the foundation than paint and decorations. To create a vision of what we want for the new room, we must first take stock of what gives value to that room.

Part of what has shattered the American Dream for many is a loss of status as defined by positions, jobs and the things that popular culture has told us are valuable. Without these, many people feel undefined because their sense of worth has come from such external trappings. As a result, many may feel that they are without value.

How you see the world and how you deal with it.
That determines your real wealth.
~Joan of Arcadia episode

To re-create our personal American Dream, a logical starting point is to redefine our own personal worth and values. We should consider that who we really are has less to do with the positions we hold, how much money we make and the things we've acquired. These are the paint and the decorations. Yes, it is perfectly okay to have these, but aren't you so much more than all of that? Doesn't your value run deeper? Perhaps it is time to redefine our worth based on our unique talents and redefine what brings meaning to our lives and the lives of others. That was an important part of what she needed to learn.

Once we have a new vision of who we want to be and what we want, we need to reassess what parts of our past support this new vision and what parts may get in the way. We need to recognize things as they are compared with where we want them to be. We need to evaluate what thoughts, behaviors, values and beliefs will serve us as we take action in a new direction and which may hold us back. This is a *huge* transition and very worthy of thoughtful consideration.

The Path of Action

Andrea had a golden opportunity to rediscover and appreciate her relationships with family members, particularly her brother, friends and new contacts at a much deeper level. Gratitude for their part in her journey was a focus that kept her moving forward. This new appreciation allowed Andrea to reformulate her own true worth, her core values and beliefs and what she could contribute to the world at large. Redefining herself based on her unique talents, strengths and the inner resources that supported Andrea's new vision helped determine the actions she needed to take in order to re-create.

To re-create our American dream, there are obvious actions needed in terms of our everyday lives: logical things like reassessing finances and budgets, considering options for employment, living arrangements and others. These are the external things that need attention.

Andrea had always been frugal and not compelled to spend money to compete with the Joneses. She did, however, need to redefine financial priorities for that time and for the future within the confines of a graduate student salary. Recommitment to the priorities of health and well-being (physically, mentally and spiritually) in addition to reducing debt and rebuilding a semblance of saving and retirement accounts were most important to her. Reconnecting with what was truly important now and for creating the future she wanted assisted in making that commitment.

Andrea had a several choices. She could re-define herself based on deeper consideration of her talents, education and core values, then decide how they may be best put to use or she could try to squeeze into a mold that no longer fit. After futile attempts to re-enter her previous profession, she chose to redefine who she was and her priorities.

Taking stock of her inner assets, vast experience in healthcare and university-level education and the value she had brought to previous organizations led her to reconfigure her resume with new confidence. She forwarded it to a broader range of potential employers than she would have considered a few months earlier. Andrea was rewarded with two solid offers for positions in positive, resourceful organizations that recognized the unique contributions she could make and valued her strengths and creativity.

Andrea accepted a position with a small research company. Initially, there was a pay cut and by some standards, a less prestigious position than what was offered by the other organization, but it was more in tune with her redefinition of herself. In retrospect, Andrea believed that realigning with her distinctive talents, experience, new sense of inner-worth and core values facilitated her growth as a scientist and contributor to the growth of the company. It also started her more solidly on the path out of survival mode and steered her onto a path more aligned with her desire to thrive at a deeper level. All of this added to an enhanced sense of self-worth.

The Inner Journey Continues

As Andrea made increasingly solid progress along the new path with a focus on the external, physical aspects of daily life, it was evident that she needed to continue to take action on a more personal, internal level.

As you begin to re-create your life and your dreams, old emotions, hurts and disempowering patterns may arise even as new challenges present themselves. Things like fear, anger, sadness and guilt may be familiar from previous stages, but may have a different intensity and underlying basis at this stage.

The strategies that were effective in previous stages will provide a good foundation for dealing with these emotions and we may need to add new tools to our tool kit. There are a few additional things we may need to work through in this stage, such as a stronger commitment to moving past victim mode, remembering fear is usually an illusion, grappling with our inner critic and letting go of the past.

Reclaiming your Power: Moving from Victim to Victor

Between stimulus and response there is a space.
In that space is our power to choose our response.
In our response lies our growth and our freedom.
~Viktor E. Frankl M.D., Ph.D.

In recounting her story about her dire financial situation, Andrea continued to lament about what went wrong until she realized that she was in blame mode, playing the victim. Tammy quickly pointed out that blame mode was hindering her growth and ability to define a better future. Andrea needed to choose a different response if she wanted to be successful. She was defining herself as powerless, at the mercy of others. She had to stop defining herself as a victim.

When we are in victim mode, we give away our power. When we choose to tap into our inner resources, we keep the power that allows us to be victorious. We need to create responses that empower us and keep us on the path of positively defining what we want. This is what helps us begin to take responsibility and gives us freedom.

Fear is a Four-Letter Word

Andrea was afraid of making the wrong choice, taking the wrong action, going in the wrong direction. She was afraid of having even more problems and more desperate circumstances. She was afraid of failing. This was a different fear than what Andrea had experienced in previous stages.

It was helpful to remember that fear is a four-letter word. Fear is often translated as **F**alse **E**xpectations **A**ppearing **R**eal or **F**alse **E**xperiences **A**ppearing **R**eal. Either way, much of what we fear is merely a mind-made illusion that we give inordinate power. Fear can be very powerful if we don't put it into perspective.

In some schools of thought, there is no such thing as failure. There is only feedback. If the result isn't what you wanted, what message, feedback, or lesson can you find that might help enhance success the next time? So, if you can't fail, what is there to fear, really?

Grappling with your Gremlin

The extent of the resistance is directly proportionate to the
importance and power of the change you want to make.
~George Leonard

If you are second-guessing your actions or doubting your abilities, you may be grappling with your gremlin. We all have a gremlin, an inner critic, who thinks its job is to keep us in the status quo and resist change.

The gremlin is often the voice that casts doubt on our ability to do something or second-guesses our choices and decisions. It is the devil/angel on each shoulder that sets up the debate in our minds and causes us to question things, even when we know deep down that something is the right thing.

The gremlin may show its face in many other ways: procrastination, wishful thinking, behaviors and attitudes that keep us stuck, all of which may happen as we prepare to re-create. Playing the victim can be a trick of the gremlin, too!

Our gremlin may have deep roots in how we perceive the world based on outmoded maps of reality and beliefs that no longer serve us that we may have taken from others. When you hear the gremlin talking, start by recognizing its voice. Next, consider ways of taking away its power and putting it in its place.

Working with your self doubts and gremlin can be a challenge and has been the subject of entire books. It is worth learning to recognize and deal with your gremlin. The best place to start is to become aware of the times you find yourself doing some of the things described above or doubting your abilities. There are a number of resources offered by The Lemonade Network that can assist you.

Letting Go of the Past and Forgiving

Part of what made it scary for Andrea to start to move ahead was that she was still attached to a past. Defining things by past expectations, priorities, values or beliefs that no longer serve us, keep us in the past. We have a choice: Stay stuck in the past and the old story *or* consider what life would be like if we let go.

Consider that there may be more advantages to letting go of the past than disadvantages. We can open to new possibilities. As we start to embrace those new possibilities we can begin to focus on how life will be enhanced, which boosts our motivation and confidence to continue onward. It creates an inner space so we can continue to redefine whatever's become undefined as circumstances present themselves.

Forgiveness is an important part of releasing the past. Failing to forgive ourselves or others only hurts the person who chooses not to forgive. Andrea continually had beaten herself up for not being a better money manager, making poor investment decisions and many other things. Before she could release the past, she needed to forgive herself. Often, it is only ourselves we need to forgive.

Forgiving is powerful and frees us up to do what we need to do. It helps us move out of victim mode. What do you need to forgive in order to redefine and re-create?

Committing to Yourself and Making it a Priority

You are worthy of having your dream, but you need to commit to doing what is needed to get there. Making a commitment to yourself is one way of honoring yourself. Making the necessary changes to begin the re-creation process must become your No. 1 priority. If your plate is already full and you don't make this your highest priority, something will always slip into its place.

By not making our agenda the top priority, we give away our power and may have to deal with changes we don't want to make. We have a choice to let others set our agenda or to take charge and set our own.

You Have More Control than You Think

As you move through this stage and beyond, consider how powerful you really are. You do have control over what you think, what you feel, what you say and what you do. All you have to do is remember to take control by using the tools you need to tap into your inner resources to access your personal power.

Continuing on the Path of Re-creation

It has now been a couple of years since Andrea started the re-creation process. The foundation she established based on the basic redefinitions from that earlier time continues to serve her as she refines her dream. The wisdom and tools she has acquired for dealing with situations and emotions have been invaluable as she continues to rebuild.

The process of re-creating her career, life and finances has been quite a journey. It has not been a straight path. The lessons learned from the previous stages and working through this stage keep Andrea moving forward as the road twists and turns. They increase her confidence so that she *can* re-create something better. More importantly, these experiences contribute to the bigger journey of her life and how she can contribute to the bigger picture.

We don't receive wisdom; we must discover it for ourselves after a journey that no one can take for us or spare us.
~Marcel Proust

Insights

As with all the stages, the insights we gain from the process, our actions and choices are what keep us moving forward. Here they help free us to re-create on our terms and accelerate our progress toward thriving versus merely surviving. Some insights and silver linings from Andrea's story:

- Our self-esteem, self worth and who we THINK we are may be tied into what others think of us, our job title, the amount of money we make and other things that aspects of society SAY we should value, such as fancy cars, or HD-TV. The realization that our worth goes so much deeper increases our awareness of who we really are at our core, our true value. The silver lining is that this awareness, if we choose to act on it, frees us to rewrite our life circumstance by redefining what is truly valuable internally and externally. When Andrea initially attempted to fit back into the "old" mold of who she "thought" she was, it didn't work. Based on a redefinition of her skills and values she started to create something much better.

- In order to really move forward, we need to let go of our "story." This includes choosing to move from victim to victor by first being aware that we are in "blame" mode. We can then realize that we really are in control of how we look at and act in the world. Letting go of negative emotions and limiting beliefs as well as forgiving others (really herself), were vital to letting go and moving forward. The silver lining here is that letting go increased Andrea's confidence in her ability to control her future instead of being at the mercy of another. It opened up a space to see opportunities and plan practical steps forward. This gave Andrea the hope that, yes, she could change things and it did wonders for her self-perception!

• The fear of moving forward and making the "wrong" choices are largely illusions we create in our minds. Dealing with this illusion and naming it for what it is takes some courage. Not dealing with it, however, means that we are likely to stay stuck in survival and fail to thrive, if we move forward at all. Here the silver lining is that we tap into the courage to be who we are and get what we want. By releasing the illusion of fear and using that courage, we have a clearer idea of the steps needed to success. Although there may be missteps along the way, learning from these, as opposed to fearing them, is a form of success and moves us closer to what we want by correcting our path. All of this can lead to increased confidence and self-perception as we continue to plan and take action.

Exercises

1. Defining or, redefining who you are: Where do you get your self-worth and self-concept? How much is from external versus internal sources? How might it be reconsidered if job, title and money were not part of the equation?

2. Personal value exercise: What are you most proud of? What talents do you possess? How might your talents and accomplishments be considered in redefining who you are and what you want? Write down five things you

do well, five things about yourself of which you are proud and five things for which you are grateful.

3. Redefine your priorities: What are your personal and financial priorities now? What priorities will be important to consider as you plan your future?

4. Practice recognizing times when you find yourself procrastinating, blaming, making excuses or saying "I can't." This may be a sign that your gremlin is in charge. Begin by naming your gremlin and giving it a funny persona that allows you to laugh in its face when it comes up with ridiculous notions like "You can't do that." Or imagine your gremlin full of hot air, blowing up like a balloon until it pops. The important key is to be aware when the gremlin is operating and prepare to grapple with it so you can move forward. This can take some practice and information in the Emotional Stimulus Package Workbook and www.LemonadeNetwork.com may help.

Going for the Gold

As you've read this chapter and worked through the exercises, you may have come to some insights about your own situation and what you need to do to continue to work through this stage and re-create your dream. What do you feel your next steps might be? What small thing can you do today, right now, that may help? Taking time to really think about these questions will pay off. Consider journaling your insights and planning your next steps. This will help you accelerate your journey.

This is an exciting stage, but also one that may take a lot of work. There are wonderful tools to add to your kit and keep you moving on the path. To really dig into progressing through this stage, you may find it helpful to download additional exercises from the Emotional Stimulus Package Workbook at www.LemonadeNetwork. com that will guide you through the process in more detail than we can do in the book.

At this stage, actively moving past any doubts, dealing with your gremlin, making thoughtful plans and taking concrete actions toward them will accelerate your progress. Tapping into The Lemonade Network's other resources such as workshops and coaching may be a logical "next step" to help you create goals and a plan for meeting them. We can provide input and guidance for dealing with your gremlin and other obstacles in a more personalized program based on your motivation and needs at this stage as well. We can help you stay motivated and reap the rewards of your work. Let us know how we can best help you by talking with one of The Lemonade Network's coaches.

Moving On

As you continue to redefine, realign and reconstruct your new life and dream, you grow into an acceptance of the path and find new energy leading to the next stage, that of hope and acceptance. Your enhanced self-perception and increasing confidence based on updated definitions of who you are and what you want provide steppingstones to this next stage.

CHAPTER 8

Stage 7: Acceptance and Hope

> **Acceptance and hope** emerge as you make use of the
> steppingstones laid in the previous stages. Ideas for
> continued action are combined with methods for tapping
> into a new sense of inner peace and joy as you anticipate
> good times again.

So, here you are! You've overcome your shock and faced the pain and guilt head on. You've wrestled the demons of anger and blame to the ground. You've bargained with the gods and lost, yet picked yourself back up again. You've been swept across the ocean of depression and loneliness to climb ashore, meeting a turning point in your life. And you have decided to design a new beginning for yourself seeing the potential for new possibilities on the horizon.

There remains one last knot to untie before you are set free. It is the lesson you came here to learn. Read the following story of Mary's liberation from her limiting beliefs and judgments that kept her in bondage to struggle and strife, and how she found happiness in surrendering these constraints. As you consider your own situation, you might ask yourself what remains in the way of your own happiness and hope. What beliefs and judgments might be holding you hostage?

Being Happy doesn't mean your life is perfect. It means you've decided to look beyond the imperfections.
~Unknown Author

Mary's Story

The ink had not yet dried on the mortgage papers for Mary and her husband's new home when the bottom dropped out of the real estate market. Mary was not overly concerned. She and her husband were experienced, competent, successful real estate agents, proud entrepreneurs with no reason to believe they would not succeed.

Always positive thinkers, they would simply ignore any negative signals, ride out the storm and manifest success and growth by working harder and smarter. With guts and spirit (and their "heads in the sand," Mary later admitted), they continued to strive and struggle, ever branching outward to try to find new ways of making income.

Mary added a skin care product distributorship, quickly becoming a top seller, as well as an entrepreneur-training business to her repertoire. Her husband worked longer hours and sought ever-more creative marketing strategies for his real estate business but the activity just wasn't happening. Buyers and sellers were hunkering down and lying low. He began to look into other means of potential quick income, online businesses, etc. but with little success.

As their focus split further, the bills continued to increase while their income decreased. Trying in vain to keep afloat by borrowing from Peter to pay Paul, their credit card debt soared to over $85,000 and their credit rating plummeted.

Mary was the only entrepreneur in her family. She was often teased for not settling down to a "real job." When the time came to pay their mortgage with non-existent funds, Mary was faced with the humiliation of having to ask her parents for money. It felt backwards, a return to a state of childlike dependence. No small matter for a proud, independent, entrepreneurial spirit.

Her husband tried to open the subject of bankruptcy as a potential solution. Mary would not hear of it. The "B" word, in her opinion, was for irresponsible shirkers or for those so frozen in the terror of insecurity that caving in was their only option. Mary saw herself as a fighter and not afraid.

Besides, she had agreements with the mortgage and credit card companies. There was a code of honor to uphold. Yet she couldn't shake the feeling that something was wrong with that logic. After all, wasn't she just ideal prey for the credit card companies? Didn't they profit by soliciting more and more credit in pursuit of higher interest paybacks from the very people who cannot afford to pay off their card balances?

Mary could feel herself digging a deeper and deeper hole with no sign of a ladder to climb out. Her mind raced day and night looking for options and solutions but none could be found. The well had dried up and there was nothing but drought in sight.

Finally the month came when Mary and her husband could not meet the mortgage payment. Nor did they have the funds the next month, and the next, until five months passed and they were facing the "F" word. Foreclosure. Mary now knew what it was like to not answer the phones for fear of a collection call. It was wearing away her resolve.

One day, hoping to catch a moment's peace from the nightmare, Mary sat down in front of her favorite movie, "Under the Tuscan Sun." She had seen it many times, but this time something in the movie pushed all of her buttons. As she watched the story of a woman finding a new life in a foreign country, she was overcome with strong emotion akin to a breaking heart and knew in that moment, beyond a shadow of a doubt, the nature of her own entrapment. It came as both a shock and a revelation.

She had always assumed her true passion was her work because she enjoyed it with enthusiasm and was good at it. But in this dawning of new awareness, with crystal clarity and a strange familiarity she realized her heart had been yearning for travel and experience in other lands and cultures.

She had indirectly sought this dream by becoming an adventurous entrepreneur but this choice was not in alignment with her core values. Rather, it was her way of conforming to the expectations she perceived others held for her. She realized for her life to thrive and flourish, she needed work not bound by location and geographical roots.

If she continued along her current path, even if they suddenly found a way out of their fiscal trap, she would never experience the kind of life she truly longed for. Unless she changed. And in this experience of reaching bottom and seeing her true reflection, she knew what to do. It was her turning point, her "aha" moment when she looked inside herself and saw she was held in bondage by her own thinking.

From Aha to Ahhh

This was Mary's first step toward the stage of acceptance. It arrives when you take yourself gently through the experience of loss and through self-reflection. You examine those beliefs taught and long held by societal conditioning and realize they no longer serve you well, and perhaps were never true in the first place. These widely acclaimed "truths" go unchallenged by the majority. They are accepted as self-evident but are often not realistic for most of the population. Here are some examples:

- A college education will give you your dream job and guaranteed success.
- People should get married young, have two children and live happily ever after.
- You need to own your own home to feel financially secure.
- More money brings more happiness.
- If you work hard and long enough at one job you will be able to retire comfortably.

When these societal rules fail to be your experience, you become disillusioned. After moving through the anger and blame, you come to see that your judgments, criticisms and fears have stemmed from those rigid rules of behavior and group perceptions that have kept you suffering, banging your head against a wall.

Many of us crucify ourselves between two thieves — regret of the
past and fear for the future.
~Fulton Oursler

Acceptance begins when it finally occurs to you that you have a choice. You can choose to uphold or shed past beliefs that tied you. It does not mean sitting down and doing nothing. But it does mean giving up the fight that keeps you suffering.

Mary realized there was only one obstacle in her way to freedom: her own thinking. She would have to discard her prejudices about bankruptcy. Break the rules she had convinced herself were her own. This would not come without a price. Her pride was at stake. She would have to form a new picture of her self worth, undefined by her previous judgments as well as what others think and say. It was a humbling but liberating experience and the relief was tremendous.

Mary made the choice to release herself from her conditioning but she still had much bushwhacking to do, figuratively and literally. As she began to clear the thoughts that blocked her path, she simultaneously began clearing out stuff from the closets, nooks and crannies of her house. This shedding of material things was both a symbolic and practical gesture that would make it easier to let go of the trappings of her former lifestyle.

Once she had given herself permission to make this shift in direction she had to face the culture that made those rules. She imagined with dread the hammering her family would give her. They would say, "We told you so" and "If only you'd gotten a real job." So before announcing any moves toward action, she sat down to reconstruct her life through research.

She consulted analysts and other professionals and with their help, had to admit their house had been a bad investment from the start. Even if they could hold on to it for another five years, it would still sell short of their original purchase price. A veritable money pit. When she finally mustered the courage to speak to her family and tell them she had decided to file bankruptcy and why, she found them unexpectedly supportive and generous in their praise for her courage and tenacity. They expressed only genuine relief and happiness for her.

The Lesson Learned

When asked the lesson she learned and advice she would give others, Mary replied, "Until you reach the point where you make your own decisions for your life you have not learned the lesson you came here for. This means not basing your life's decision on what others are doing or what you think others would approve. Learn your lesson now. But, if not ready to learn now, I hope you will experience enough pain or discomfort in the future to learn your lesson."

If you have not yet come to your "aha" moment, be patient. Be open to investigation and it will come when you are ready. Listen to your inner guidance system. After a loss, your emotions are in a heightened state and can teach you much about yourself. Pay attention to the actions, places, people and things that give you comfort, or moments of joy and laughter. Notice small coincidences that are actually serendipitous opportunities.

Follow thoughts that bring you a sense of peace. Linger there and study them. Conversely, watch thoughts that bring you pain and simply notice them. It is unlikely you will ever return to the original carefree, untroubled you that existed before this tragedy, but you will find a way to a happier you.

When you do reach this stage of acceptance, you understand there has been a lesson learned, and you will be able to look back without regret. It does not mean you have found "happily ever after" or there will be no more pain.

Since the decision to cut her losses and change tracks, Mary's new world is still sprinkled with brief moments of intense pain. The memories of the struggle are still fresh in her mind. But she has learned to seek what nourishes her. To allow herself time to sit with the lesson, to separate from the intensity of change and relax with a good book, a movie, or simply pause for rest and contemplation.

One of the beneficial side effects of this stage of acceptance is the noticeable physical change. You will hear your friends and loved ones say, "What have you been doing? You look different. You look great!" When you shed your false perceptions, you no longer carry heavy burdens and no longer wear your mask of stress. You not only look different but also feel more whole and wholesome and it shows.

Opening Your Mind to the Possibilities

Acceptance does not mean you sit back and wait for something to happen to you. Mary has a new direction now. She has stepped onto a new path with new plans for her future. She has decided her work is not her passion but her work can finance her passion. The difference has opened up a new world of possibilities and freedom. She began to hunt for a job that would create much less stress and pay enough to support a rental condo with a little left to save for future travels. Never again will she buy bigger than her means or play the credit card game for prestige or approval.

Accepting the way things are and the changes you must make to move forward not only opens your mind, but the world around you begins to change before your eyes. In this down economy, many fledgling businesses are actually thriving. As values change, market demand shifts.

Bicycle and used-car businesses are growing as people seek reliable, lower-cost transportation. College enrollments are increasing as people go back to school to gain more training and make good use of their layoff time. Self-help skills are in great demand as people learn to build things, grow their own gardens and look into collaborative pursuits. These new directions are bringing great benefits to trade schools, organic farms, coaching and training businesses and home-building supply stores.

Are you ready to shift with the changing tide of the times? Can you open your mind to the notion that you are indeed creative, resourceful and whole? Can you begin to see there are new possibilities, new opportunities, new ideas that may excite and ignite you with joy and bring new prosperity to your life?

Giving and Receiving

After finally filing bankruptcy and accepting whatever was to come next, Mary and Steve were astonished at the turn-around in their previously luckless situation. A job landed in Mary's lap and her husband escrowed a large real estate transaction. Mary's family gifted her with a long-awaited new laptop computer. It seemed as though abundance began to pour back into their lives, like a cool drink of water after a long dry spell.

An indicator of reaching the stage of acceptance is the attitude of receiving. When Mary stopped beating herself up, unloaded what was no longer hers to carry and began to nurture herself, she became open to receiving and her world became abundant.

When we are hard on ourselves, we forget to ask for help. At a very young age, many of us are taught it is better to give than receive and this belief is strongly reinforced in our culture with holiday gift-giving traditions. When we give, we actually receive and when we receive, we are also giving. We do this by providing those who give to us a safe way of expressing their inherent goodness and kindness. And they feel better about themselves.

As people move forward from loss, they find their friends ready and waiting to support and give in numerous ways. What is unique and comforting about this economic crisis is we are all in it together. We do not need to feel alone in this collective experience of loss. Allowing others to give provides a venue for sharing in the human experience that otherwise is not always available.

It creates a bonding experience that strengthens communities. Perhaps you have witnessed this outpouring of support through memorial funds, barn-raising or fund-raising events in your community when someone has experienced a loss, such as a house fire, expensive illness or the death of a loved one.

In this time of economic crisis, many people have found creative ways to give back to their communities. There is a collaborative movement to simplify our lives, return to the basics and work together to provide a better way of life for all. Community gardens are cropping up all over the country. There are neighborhood garage sales, do-it-yourself workshops and growing support of local farmers markets.

In a small northwestern town, a retired gentleman felt compelled to do something for those in his community who had lost their jobs through layoffs and cutbacks. He bought bushels of lentils, had them wrapped in 1-pound bags, attached instructions for how to cook them and left them on a first-come, first-served basis at a local café. It was such a big hit and he so enjoyed the response, he repeated the event.

In the Acceptance stage we learn to ask for help when needed. Once open to receiving, abundance pours in. With abundance comes gratitude and with gratitude comes an attitude of wanting to give back. You will find yourself looking for ways to help others and will personally experience the healing power in such gestures.

Have you accepted anyone's help lately? If not, remember that asking is giving and try it. You will be amazed and gratified at what happens next.

> *We are all angels who only have one wing.*
> *That's why we need each other to fly.*
> ~"All Angels"   by Karen Drucker

Hopefulness

Once you have come to accept what is, learned the lesson, detached from your past fears and failures and taken your first steps forward, you are ready to enter the Hope stage. There is a tiny flicker of happiness inside you beginning to warm into a burning flame. It is as though the clouds of pain and suffering agree to part and make way for blue sky and sun. There will be other rainy days ahead. They will come and go as a fact of life. But for now, in this moment, it is enough to see clear skies and to choose to notice the feeling with appreciation.

Hope is not wishful thinking but envisioned success. Hope is the place your mind goes when it sees possibilities. You have begun once again to dream your life so that you can live your dream, your unique and personal version of the American Dream. Revised, renewed and re-created by you, for you.

There are those who would advise against false hope. These are the perennial pessimists prevalent in our media and our social groups who are really in the game to distract us from where truth resides in our inner guidance. Many times they are disguised as caring relatives who mean to protect you from further disillusionment and pain. Bless their good intentions but move onward with your own sense of hopefulness in spite of their advice.

False hope is wishful thinking. It is based on non-responsibility. Valid hope means you are ready again to invest in your future for which you take full responsibility. The game of your life is back in your hands and you are ready to play again, with new strategies and starting from a new position of enlightened advantage.

The very least you can do in your life is to figure out what you hope for. And the most you can do is live inside that hope. Not admire it from a distance, but live right in it, under its roof.
~Barbara Kingsolver

Insights

- To some, reaching a true state of acceptance would seem like giving up, but actually it might more accurately be described as "giving in," or inward giving. It is the state of allowing your truth within you to preside over your choices, rather than giving up your truth to something or someone outside of yourself. Acceptance is an action of great courage and strong adherence to the truth. It is when you become fully responsible for your feelings, emotions and decisions.
- The hardest thing to accept is change, yet the only thing that doesn't change is that nothing remains the same. Life is change. Crisis is change. The best we can do is try and take the changes in stride as we move forward on our path of learning to live a meaningful life.
- Acceptance often happens when we become still and listen to our inner voice and hopefulness speaks of forward

movement. When we hope we make the choice to look ahead with curiosity and joy rather than fearfulness or dread about what will be around the corner. It is similar to the anticipation of unwrapping wondrous surprises on Christmas morning. Starting a new job, finding a new relationship, moving to a new home, making a fresh start, are hopeful experiences of change. None of these are easy changes and you do not have to navigate the unknown without a partner. Remember, we are on this journey together. There are resources, supportive tools and ideas, and your biggest fans at www.LemonadeNetwork.com.

Exercises
It All Begins With Your Dream

1. Describe your desired future as though you were reciting a dream. Put all the details you can envision into it. There is no right, wrong or ridiculous. Let your imagination go and don't be afraid to think big.

Vision Board

2. Find pictures, draw, or paint to represent what you want to manifest in your life. Your ideal scene. Put the pictures on a bulletin board, wall or your computer desktop where you can see them daily. When your intention is full of trust and expectancy, you will reach your goals sooner.

Create Social Support

3. It is important at this time to seek out and create new relationships that foster your growth and encourage the changes you want to make in your life. You have already released beliefs and resentments that held you back. Now release with loving acceptance, those people in your life who continue to hold you back. Allow them their beliefs but don't buy into them. You have chosen to live outside their box. You are creating a new product, a new and improved you.

4. It is time to make a change in your social investment fund. This means looking for new social experiences, new friends, church, clubs or groups you have always wanted to join but did not while you were bound by the thought, "What would my friends and relatives say?" Realize you have chosen a new path. A path without past constraints. You will need someone to walk along with you and it very likely will be someone new.

    Don't worry about your old social attachments. Hopefully, they will understand. Or you may re-establish a deeper and more beneficial relationship later on as they see you recovering and leaving them behind. This is, for some, the hardest step to take and requires great faith and trust in yourself.
    The stage of Acceptance and Hope is not always clearly recognized. How do you know when you have arrived? What does it feel like?

You Are Here

In that space between sleep and full awakening to the dawn, there is no remembrance of the pain of the past, struggle of the present or worries for the future. It is the moment when hope flickers and joy lies waiting. Warm, secure, basking in the love of life, at this moment it is easy to feel young, innocent, reborn, excited about a new day and all that it will bring. This is where you truly belong, in this state of anticipation and expectancy. When you can create this feeling, you are experiencing acceptance and hope. When you can make it a habitual part of your life, congratulations! You have arrived! Now, may you never be the same.

Moving On

Now that you made it through the stages, let's take a look at the big picture and see where we can go together.

CHAPTER 9

Seeing the Forest for the Trees

Hope is like the sun which, as we journey towards it, casts the shadow of our burden behind us.
~Samuel Smiles

By now, you've had the chance to consider where you are with respect to grieving the loss of your American Dream. This in and of itself is a start on your journey toward hope! Perhaps you've gained some insight into working through that stage and considered how shifting your reality is an important part of the process. In each of the stages, we suggest that you have a choice and the opportunity to consider small, reasonable steps to help you reach your goals. You may have outlined a plan and started to take some initial action. All of these insights, shifts, choices and small steps can be used to create the foundation on which to rebuild your personal American Dream. Up to this point, it may have been a challenge to see the forest for the trees. It may be time to consider the forest, in other words, get a glimpse of a bigger picture.

Where have we been?

Let's take a look back at some of the things we have covered as we've worked through the seven stages.

The losses that have come with the current economic situation are similar to the loss of a loved one in that we are going through a process of grieving. While each stage of grief appears to be separate, they are intertwined and we may visit the stages out of order. We may visit some more than once. The good news is that, as you work through the stages, you learn and acquire tools that can keep you moving forward.

There are some common themes that weave across the stages including awareness, self-perception and our sense of control and choice.

Our losses initially are a blow to our self-concept and we question our self-worth. In addition, we sense that things are beyond our control. Some of this may be unconscious. In the first four stages in particular, our reactions - shock, denial, pain, guilt, anger, bargaining and depression - are part of our coping mechanism as we work on sorting things out. They are a part of an undercurrent that comes when questioning our self-worth and our perceived lack of control. Consider Carol in Chapter 3. Her self-esteem was compromised when she lost her job and couldn't get back on her feet. Her self-concept was tied into her prior professional success.

Part of the transformation as we work through the first four stages involves regaining a positive self-image. It also entails finding a new perspective about our situation and ways of taking control of it. The question is, how do we do this?

Common Threads

The aim of life is to live, and to live means to be aware, joyously, drunkenly, serenely and divinely aware.
~Henry Miller

Throughout the book you may have picked up on some themes that appeared in many chapters. Two prominent and important ideas are those of awareness and choice. You may have noticed that exercises and questions in the chapters have heightened your awareness of issues at a given stage.

Modern philosopher Ken Wilber states that "Awareness in and of itself is transformational." The beauty of being more conscious of our emotions, actions and reactions is that it helps us consider options for responding. Sometimes our choices seem subtle. Even *not* doing something is a choice. It may *appear* that we have no alternatives, but often all we need do is step back and consider what options we really do have. Here is where a coach or neutral third party can help you brainstorm and follow through with new options. Recognizing that we do have choices is an important step toward regaining control.

In each chapter, there are examples of important decisions that were made to do something different. In each case, there was a new awareness that helped the person be open to new choices.

Chris's story in Chapter 2 is a common example. He suffered with extreme daily anxiety just trying to keep his financial balls in the air rather than admit he had a problem and needed help. Once Chris acknowledged that his life wasn't working, he opened himself up to finding a solution. His life changed almost immediately and the anxiety, while not gone, was significantly less.

Adam's move toward success in Chapter 3 started with his awareness of his situation and, based on that, reclaiming his power through taking action. He thought through his predicament and chose to become proactive. This provided him with at least the perception that he had "control" of things that allowed him to move forward with plans to change his direction.

In Chapter 4, as Cathy became aware of the basis of her anger, she realized she could use it productively or allow it to destroy her health. She opted to work through her anger rather than stay stuck in it. She decided to remove herself from the emotional triggers that kept her in battle with herself. She chose to surround herself with an environment of activities; work and people that made her feel worthwhile, productive and loved. Her move, though potentially impractical from a financial viewpoint, allowed her the space to take responsibility for and control her emotions. Once she realized that she had a right to create the preferences in her life, it became easier. Without anger for a partner, avenues of opportunity opened up for her new business and it steadily grew. Her focus became clearer. Her heart opened to provide space for abundance once again.

When Jerry was experiencing depression and loneliness in Chapter 5 after being laid off from his job of 39 years, he had a choice. He could remain indefinitely in that valley where everything looked hopeless or he could decide to change his circumstances. As Jerry worked through the stages of the death of his American Dream, he became aware of the hidden potential in turning his hobby into a profession. This worked out very well for him and created a lot of happy new customers who needed his services. He not only made a dramatic difference in his own life, he also touched many other lives in the process. Realize that Jerry's circumstances did not change overnight. It was a step-by-step process that started very slowly and gradually picked up momentum, but it would never have changed if he had not taken the opportunity to change it.

Taking the Reins

There is nothing either good or bad, but thinking makes it so.
~William Shakespeare

In the stories in the first four stages, consider how the awareness and choices led each of these people to greater control of their situation. This leads us to another of the common themes that appears throughout the book, namely how we perceive things.

We sometimes THINK we have no control over a situation. Throughout life, there are events and circumstances that arise which are not what we want and aren't pleasant. The results that come from these are related to the choices we make about how to respond to them based on a simple equation:

Circumstance (or event) + Response = Result (or outcome)

We may or may not be able to alter the event or circumstance. We do, however, have options for how we think about the situation. This greatly influences how we respond. Recognizing that we can choose our thoughts helps us manage our response. We can control the perception of the result at the very least. Some thoughts and decisions also give us control over the circumstance or event!

As we pointed out in the various stories, the key to exercising our options is to first be aware. From there, we can consider how to think about things and respond. Now, we may not *like* the result that we get from our choice of response. This doesn't mean we've failed, but rather that we need to take the result as feedback, learn something from it and consider other alternatives in the future. Again, this helps us re-establish a semblance of control.

The bottom line when working through the stages (the first four in particular) means that at some point we recognize that staying where we are is more painful than moving forward in a different direction. Being conscious of the circumstances, thoughts, emotions and reactions that are not serving us, allows us to take advantage of new ways of dealing with them and take control. It help us progress on the path with new confidence.

Moving Toward Hope and Acceptance

While progressing through the first four stages, the practice of making choices based on increased awareness starts to help us feel better about ourselves and life in general as we emerge from these more "survival" stages. It opens us up to the "aha" of the Upward Turn with the start of some confidence, renewed energy and sense of a bit more control.

Marsha's Upward Turn in Chapter 6 could only begin when her reality snapped and allowed in the light of awareness. It wasn't pleasant and it didn't feel good, but as a result, she began to take one small, progressive action after another including: finding housecleaning clients, dramatically scaling back her expenses and negotiating with creditors while she mounted a full-scale job search. Even though the outcome was unclear, with each step she found a new perspective and began to find her footing again, even though the path was rocky and steep. Her energy returned and continuing the climb didn't seem so difficult.

As we practice awareness and make decisions from that awareness, the process of self-discovery helps build our self-esteem.

Building on the insights from the Upward Turn and previous stages enhances our courage to make additional plans and take some new risks and actions as we redefine our value, who we are and what we want. It boosts our esteem as we realize a new sense of worth and that we do have more control than we thought.

In Chapter 7, Andrea realized that it was necessary to redefine herself in terms of her core values and skills. She opted to build on these instead of trying to squeeze back into a mold that no longer fit. This gave her courage to explore a wider range of employment options. As she reconnected with a deeper definition of self and went for interviews, her self-perception improved and she felt much more in control of her destiny. This gave her hope for the future and helped her emerge from mere survival.

The increased energy from stages 5 and 6, together with continued self-discovery that comes with practicing awareness, prepares us for some of the deeper challenges that we may have as we move toward acceptance and hope.

If we were to conclude from Chapter 8 that Mary's important decision was to file bankruptcy to bring relief to her pain, we would be missing the point. The more important choice that Mary had to make was to let go of the limiting beliefs that had directed her along her life's journey. She had been unaware that these beliefs were always guiding her choices. They were really not her beliefs and consequently had constrained her happiness. She kept running into walls until she chose to follow her own inner guidance. When she took complete responsibility for her decision, she realized she had full control of her life and the effect was liberation and hope.

By the time we reach the last stage, the concept of acceptance has expanded beyond acceptance of the original circumstances. It goes beyond acknowledging the loss and realization that things will never be the same. It is now about accepting the journey and the transformation on the way to a new dream. By now we appreciate that continuing to practice awareness, considering our thoughts (perceptions) and making new choices translates into increased courage. It increases our confidence that we can create something better. The last stage is also about acknowledging the immense progress we've made.

So, working through the stages brings us somewhat full circle. We go from the loss of esteem and confidence to finding new strength, esteem and confidence.

Only in growth, reform, and change, paradoxically enough,
is true security to be found.
~Anne Morrow Lindbergh

Other Common Threads

You may have noticed some additional themes that many stages have in common. One that is frequently mentioned is that the stages are not necessarily linear. In other words, you may not experience them in a specific order and you may weave in and out of them more than once.

We've noted several times that there is no set time limit or duration for the stages. It is your journey on your time. Do consider, however, that being stuck, particularly in the earlier stages, does have potential drawbacks and may adversely influence your health. If you feel that you are stuck, working with one of our coaches or other professionals may help you move past whatever obstacle is inhibiting you. The Lemonade Network Coaches and programs can provide you with help and ideas on how to move forward.

You've probably noticed, too, that fear, anger, other negative emotions and limiting beliefs are mentioned in many of the stages. They may manifest differently in different stages. They may have a different intensity or feel that will require different tools to help work through them. Again, help is available.

Exercises

Here are a few questions to consider.

1. What have you become more aware of as you've worked through various stages? Has this awareness influenced your thoughts or choices? How?

2. What thoughts, actions, decisions or shifts have helped boost your confidence and regain a sense of control?

3. What positive things have resulted from working through the stages so far? How have they helped you understand the "big picture" and give you hope for the future?

Moving On

Sometimes when we are embroiled in our daily tasks and in working through the emotions and challenges at each stage, it may be difficult to "see the forest for the trees." By revisiting the insights and choices of various people throughout the stages, perhaps you have a clearer idea of the forest, that bigger picture for yourself. Their successes at each stage should give you hope. Yes, you can do it, too!

If we look at the big picture, we can see that, indeed, working through each of the stages does provide steppingstones that we can use to re-create and rebuild our dreams, if we choose to actively embrace the journey. These steppingstones increase our awareness and open us to new choices. They help us take control and lead to improved self-perception as we build on our successes. The process gives us the opportunity to re-discover ourselves and re-create in ways we may not have imagined before. Isn't that wonderful!

A final common thread linking the stories of those who embraced the journey and used the stages as steppingstones is a bit subtle at first glance. When we look back at them, we see that something *positive* came from each situation and stage. Despite the circumstances and challenges, our heroes and heroines grew personally and created a more solid footing as they took each step along the path to a new dream.

So, take heart! Yes, you can do it! Step by step...one step at a time.....

CHAPTER 10

Rebuilding your American Dream

The future belongs to those who believe in the beauty
of their dreams.
~Eleanor Roosevelt

Where to Start?

You need to start by assessing where you are in the stages of grief, at least most of the time. The concepts presented in each chapter can help you get through your current stage and set you up for the next one. If you've made it through the stages in Chapters 7 and 8, it may be time to move forward in earnest to rebuild your dream. Consider your current situation. Now consider what you really want for the future and how that will be different from your current circumstance. Is there an opportunity to rebuild at this time?

As discussed in Chapter 7, in order to remodel a room or rebuild your dream you need to prepare and make a plan before taking action. Without these, you are less likely to be successful. Rebuilding your dream will mean you'll need to prepare and plan the financial aspects.

As pointed out in Chapter 1, the preparation and planning also need to include the mental and emotional aspects of rebuilding the dream. This part of the rebuilding process is what sets the stage for the successful rebuilding of not only financial assets, but for true abundance that goes beyond. For many, spiritual preparation and planning go hand-in-hand with the mental, emotional and financial aspects. Of course, there is always a choice of whether to rebuild or not.

What it Will Take to Rebuild

Like remodeling a home, rebuilding your dream takes time and energy. It requires a vision of what needs to be different and a basic concept of what it will look like completed. Both projects require that you consider what things are truly valuable and how high they sit on the priority list. You'll need to make decisions about competing options and priorities after considering the pros and cons.

Both have their good times and their challenges. You may need to do some tearing down of the old to make space for the new. You may need to acquire new tools that will help you get the job done effectively. Both require a commitment of resources, whether internal, external or both.

Both hold the promise, but not the guarantee that, when all is said and done, things will be better. At the very least, through both, you will have learned something about yourself that can serve you in future situations.

Are you ready and willing to commit to rebuilding given that you'll need to do all of the above? If not, what is standing in your way? How will you work through the obstacles?

Even if you are on the right track,
you'll get run over if you just sit there.
~Will Rogers

First Things First - Make a Plan, Stan!

When you are ready to rebuild, have a vision and a plan for what you want to accomplish. Preparation is the key to success.

Your plan needs to:

- Include a defined goal and time frame
- Include initial steps to get you started and at least a draft of the milestones and incremental steps needed to reach them
- Anticipate obstacles and how you will work around them
- Be *yours*. No one else can do it for you.

Creating a realistic plan comes from anticipating the obstacles, using the tools and resources as you redefine whatever's become undefined. It will boost your confidence as you see the plan take shape. Making a plan can help you counter the anxiety that may come with moving forward.

It gives you a road map and a focus to facilitate your journey, but it must be *your* plan, not what someone else thinks you should do or plans for you. It cannot be a plan based on how someone else sees your worth and value, but one that honors your deeper sense of value and true abundance. As you create your game plan, there are a few things to keep in mind:

- Rome wasn't built in a day! Start with small, achievable, realistic steps. It really is the little things that lay a solid foundation. Even if you only rehearse the way you will do something, it is a start.

- Consider what obstacles stand in your way, and then identify the tools, emotional support and physical support you'll need to overcome those obstacles.
- Make your goals SMART: Specific, Measurable, Achievable, Realistic and Timely.

Set some realistic time frames but don't take action until you're prepared. Action without preparation will compromise your success. When setting dates, consider what will be needed to meet that deadline, anticipate what obstacles you might encounter and make a plan for dealing with them.

As described in Chapter 7, several things must be in place before taking action to help move you toward success.

- You need a vision of what you want and who you are or want to be. What do you want? Who do you want to be?
- You need to be committed and the project needs to be your highest priority. If you aren't committed to rebuilding, why not? Is it a priority? What else are you committed to that has a higher priority? Is it worth switching priorities at this time?

Keep Moving

As you take action and rebuild, there are five basic things that you'll continually do.

- **Remove the debris as you go**. As with the room remodel, at each stage you've needed to tear down something that no longer served you – an emotion, an attitude, a limiting belief. Working through the exercises may help you clear the debris, making room for the new structure. As you continue rebuilding, you will most likely encounter additional debris that needs to be removed before continuing. You now have some basic tools for dealing with the debris.

• **Refocus as needed.** We have choices on how to focus our energies and thoughts on what is truly important and empowering. Occasionally we may get distracted and fall back into the old patterns of thinking and behaving that didn't serve us. Refocus on your vision, your plan. Adjust the plan if needed but continually refocus on what you want to keep moving forward. Recommitting and refocusing go hand-in-hand to moving you toward success.

• **Restructure** from the new foundation of inner strength, new values and self-worth using your unique talents and ideas. It is a constant process as you acquire new tools.

• **Remain flexible.** Life happens. Sometimes things don't turn out quite the way we've planned despite our preparation and best intentions. If we consider there is no failure, only feedback, we can remain flexible. Take the lesson and apply it to the next step.

• **Reach out.** There is support available every step of the way. Not the "bail out" type, but the type that can keep you on track, stay committed and reach your goals. Keep checking back with The Lemonade Network at www.LemonadeNetwork.com. You'll continue to find new friends and helpful resources there.

The Bigger Picture

Again consider our analogy of remodeling a room in a house. As that room takes shape in its new form, it affects the rest of the house, doesn't it? By taking things step-by-step to redefine and rebuild your dream, you have a profound impact on re-creating the dream for the bigger network of family, friends, neighbors and the nation. As we answer the call to shift our consciousness, values and priorities as individuals, we contribute to the collective moving forward toward a new American Dream.

A room is part of a bigger structure like a home and as it changes form during the remodel, so does the home. As we re-create and work through the stages as individuals, it helps re-create the dreams for others in our lives and for those we'll never meet.

Exercises

1. Sketch out an initial SMART goal for what you want. It should be something that is future-oriented compared with something you want to avoid. For example, a forward-looking goal would state that you have a certain amount of money saved on a specific date to pay an upcoming bill. An example of an avoidance goal would be "I don't want to have my check bounce." Be sure that your goal is consistent with your values and priorities. Give it a try!

   S = **specifically** what do you want? Remember to keep it **simple**.
   M = **measurable**: How will you know you've gotten your goal?

A = is it **achievable?**

R = is it **realistic** and **responsible?**

T = in what **time** frame? Is it **toward** what you want?

2. What is one small step that you can take right now, today, toward making your goal? What obstacles do you foresee in taking your baby step? In achieving your goal? How might you turn them into steppingstones to get what you want?

Onward!

Congratulations. If you've made it this far you probably have a better understanding of why you've been feeling off balance and emotional. You've been guided through the grieving process and have practiced some exercises that have gotten you closer to the re-creation of a new life. The insights and tools learned are yours forever to rely upon whenever new opportunities are ready to be seized. Use them! It's recommended that you go back through the book and pick out exercises that you may have skipped over the first time through. Because this process is non-linear, what was relevant to you on the first reading may have changed, and vice versa. Information you had previously skimmed could be most useful now or at a later date.

Remember that you're not alone on this journey. Take advantage of the many resources available to help you. You'll find a list of them in the Resources section of this book. Join a support group. If there's not one in your neighborhood, start one. Or find a community online that addresses your core needs. Talk to your family and friends. They may be yearning to express their feelings to someone like you. Find a coach or a mentor. Attend a workshop. And don't forget to visit us at www.LemonadeNetwork.com. The opportunities for support are endless.

Again, congratulations! No matter how large or small your progress has been, it's important to acknowledge yourself for taking the initiative toward change. Acknowledgment and celebration can be powerful, positive motivators for taking the next step and then the next. After all, it just takes one baby step at a time to reach the top of the mountain. You're on your way!

Moving On

Now, it is time to embrace the opportunities. The death of the American Dream has given birth to a new future. As individuals and as a nation, we need to learn from our experiences to create a life that embraces our new priorities.

There is strength and encouragement in numbers as your family and friends move together toward a richer America.

CHAPTER 11

Embrace the Opportunities

As you begin the re-creation process, take advantage of the unique opportunities this economic crisis has given us. Life has a way of handing out lessons whether we are looking for them or not. It is time to release the past and embrace the opportunities of the future.

Sometimes we stare so long at a door that is closing
that we see too late the one that is open.
~Alexander Graham Bell

The Opportunity to Talk

The subject of money seems to be the last taboo subject in this country. The fact that the latest financial crisis has affected nearly every American provides the opportunity to openly discuss finances. Today it is more socially acceptable to talk about money. Take advantage of it.

The No. 1 reason for divorce is money. The most common cause of stress is money. Why? It is the lack of communication. Couples can and will disagree on some money issues but generally it is not the disagreement that causes disconnect but rather the absence of constructive discussions on budgets and expenditures. When you feel alone, stress is magnified. Sharing your fears with a spouse, family member or friend can reduce stress. There is power in numbers. That person may not have the answers but sometimes just a kind word that helps you get from one day to the next.

There are horrific stories of men who kill their entire families rather than face financial ruin. They didn't feel they could talk about the truth or seek help from anyone. The pain was internalized until it defined them. One such tragedy is too many.

Money does not define us. Take this opportunity to bring money into your conversations with family and friends. Parents, talk to your children about money, saving and budgets. Couples, keep the lines of communication open and deal with issues as they arise. Friends, be honest with each other about what you can and cannot afford to do.

The Opportunity to Reprioritize

As your particular financial reality becomes apparent and it is clear you need to make changes, now is the time you can reprioritize your life. Schedules keep our days busy, but do they reflect our priorities? Don't answer the question too quickly. Read it again. Really think about it. It is a deep question.

What are your priorities? Can you clearly define them? It is very easy to get caught up in the day-to-day craziness of life and lose sight of the big picture. This most recent crisis has made a lot of people sit down and re-evaluate their lives. What is most important? What can we live with and what can we live without? "Living without" seems to be the order of the day. This is not necessarily a bad thing.

Schedules are crammed with fillers. Fillers can be any number of things but they do have one thing in common. They help you avoid what you should be focusing on today. Days, weeks, months, even years pass in a blur because our days are filled with so many activities we get carried along with the tide. Even our children need day planners.

These fillers sap not only our money but also our energy. Many do not necessarily coincide with our priorities. As you evaluate your life, goals and aspirations, clearly define your priorities. As you rock back and forth on the porch of reflection later in life, what will you remember? What will you regret?

If you eliminate just some of the fillers in your life, you will have more time to spend on what is truly important to you.

What are your fillers?

The Opportunity to Find Your Passion

Job loss can be financially and emotionally devastating. Yet that loss brings opportunity. Americans spend an enormous amount of their time at work and nearly half of them are unhappy. If you are at a crossroads in your profession, maybe it is time to consider a change.

Change can be scary. But what is scarier? Working your entire life in a job you hate or taking a chance at finding your passion? If you have lost your job, take the opportunity to look in different directions. You can take a different path. Open your mind to the possibilities. You don't have to do what you have always done.

If you are in a profession that doesn't fulfill you, now may or may not be the best time to look for another one. It can, however, be a time for reflection. What if you lost your job tomorrow? What would you do? What would you *want* to do?

Have you taken the time to reprioritize your life? Does your current profession align with those new priorities?

Opportunities to find deeper powers within ourselves come when life seems most challenging.
~Joseph Campbell

The Opportunity for Gratitude

Gratitude is an emotion that can completely fill you. As financial pressures continue to mount, it may be harder to bring this emotion to the surface. Yet, your happiness may depend on it. As the country begins to downsize and Americans are living with less, we can choose to be unhappy with what we don't have or be grateful for what we do have.

Every day is an opportunity to be grateful for something. The hug from a child, the gentle touch of a spouse, a nuzzle from a beloved pet. At the end of the day, you can reflect on all of the bad things that happened that day, or you can find one thing to be grateful for. Maybe you can find more than one thing.

You Have the Power

You have the power to control your destiny. Take the reins. Re-create your American dream.

About the Authors

Andrea C. Skelly, Ph.D., MPH

Age: 52

Hometown: Kirkland, Washington

After being fired from a waitressing job, Andrea Skelly trusted her intuition to start a career in medical ultrasound when few had heard of it. And when an "evil dean from hell" forced her to go back to school for advanced degrees, she trusted again.

Skelly has been teaching and advising at the graduate and university levels for more than 20 years, training over 400 students for positions in a specialized medical field, some of whom have won national awards. She has chaired a national organization, sat on the boards of directors of several national professional societies and a business. She had served as a representative from her profession providing input on a National Institute of Health consensus document and to U.S. Food and Drug Administration meetings.

In addition to overseeing two publications, Skelly is director of evidence-based practice for a research consulting company and teaches yoga and personal growth workshops.

Skelly considers her survival skills as most relevant to her current work and aspirations: surviving two divorces, a Ph. D., near-financial ruin and numerous other life challenges. Her health care and research backgrounds, coupled with her trainings in health coaching, hypnosis, yoga and ancient Hawaiian Huna, help her empower people to take control of their lives by guiding them to ask pertinent questions, discover personally effective tools and locate their inner resources to create the lives they want.

Catherine Lidster, GCFP

Age: 54

Hometown: Sandpoint, Idaho

Catherine E. Lidster credits death, divorce and destruction as her most powerful teachers during the last decade.

Her house burned down while her mother lay dying from an accident caused by hospital staff negligence. Her husband walked out on their 32-year marriage, which abruptly dissolved their lifelong partnership in their jointly owned clinic. She found herself suddenly starting her own private practice from scratch and a zero bank balance in a down economy. Her kids have left the nest. Friends are either dying of fatal illnesses or have died.

Lidster had no choice but learn how to re-create her reality by shifting her perceptions, and shed the old to walk in the new with grace and beauty. She is using 30 years of experience in the alternative health and healing field in her new business as a combination Feldenkrais® and Nutrition Response practitioner and health coach.

She is a walking example to her clients of how to create your life in alignment with your integrity and true self, and how sharing your spirit creates loving and uplifting relationships.

Lidster has a Bachelor of Science in Health Education, Public Health Science and Teaching, plus many years of post-graduate studies in alternative health sciences. She lives in Sandpoint, Idaho.

Danny Fitzpatrick, MPA

Age: 57

Hometown: Sedona, Arizona

Danny Fitzpatrick has more than 20 years experience in corporate marketing as a video and event producer, but considers two layoffs and an unexpected eviction as the foundation for her current life calling as an entrepreneur and professional life coach.

These events gave Fitzpatrick the opportunity to use her innate ability to make "a silk purse from a sow's ear," as one of her former managers put it, reinventing herself and her career goals.

In early 1998 she turned an eviction from a rental home into a financial success story when she bought residential property in the San Francisco market just before values skyrocketed. When she sold the home in 2007, the value had nearly quadrupled.

As a video and event producer, Fitzpatrick contracted with top companies such as Sun Microsystems Inc., Apple Computer Inc., Oracle Corp., Bank of America Corp., Sony Corp., Shaklee Corp. and others. She has a Bachelor of Arts in Broadcast Communications from San Francisco State University.

Fitzpatrick has used adversity to train for new opportunities. She earned a Master in Organizational Management, became a certified advanced meeting facilitator and a certified hospice volunteer.

She believes these skill sets assist in her role as a coach, helping people lead well-balanced lives based on supporting their core values and purpose. Fitzpatrick is an independent film fan, a member of the National Ayurvedic Medical Association and lives in Sedona, Arizona.

Jeanette Carter

Age: 66

Hometown: Oklahoma City, Oklahoma

Jeanette Carter is a self-made woman who started her 30-year career in corporate America by teaching herself programming languages at home at night with books from the company library. When this data entry operator "blew the lid off the scale" on the programming aptitude test, she was immediately transferred into the programming department as a trainee.

Carter worked her way up through the ranks to programming manager, spending the last 13 years of her career at Wal-Mart corporate headquarters where she was the project leader for many major projects.

Her lifelong interest in illness prevention and natural approaches to health led her to start her own wellness business in 1994 while still working full-time. Five years later she retired from "corporate America" to focus on her wellness business, remarried and relocated with her new husband.

A certified wellness educator and professional health coach, Carter credits her childhood with establishing a love of nature, fresh food and an active lifestyle. The harvest from a very large family garden was sold to numerous grocery stores and restaurants for many years. Carter still had enough time and energy to play basketball in junior and senior high school, as well as reign as homecoming queen in her senior year.

Mother, grandmother and great-grandmother, Carter lives in Oklahoma City, Oklahoma, with her husband, Jerry, and their blended families. She entertains no thoughts of retiring because she's too focused on being a calming influence to help people become emotionally grounded as they rebuild their lives after loss.

Kathy Pandich

Age: 44

Hometown: Jacksonville, Florida

After 14 years in the corporate world that included high-level project management experience with two Wall Street firms, Pandich counts her blessings daily. The last Wall Street firm she worked for was Cantor Fitzgerald on the 103rd floor of the World Trade Center. Had she not quit her job to move to Ohio and have a baby, her name would have been among the friends and colleagues she lost on 9/11.

Pandich counts as another painful lesson spending too many years as an entrepreneur with the wrong partner. She worked 20-hour days and invested a significant amount of money only to lose it all and nearly her health. The experience proved to her that life needs balance.

Now, as a corporate health coach and speaker with her own consulting business, she believes her life experience gives her a clearer perspective in helping individuals and businesses place more emphasis on their health and the health of their employees.

Pandich has a Bachelor of Science in Marketing and Communications and lives in Jacksonville, Florida, with her husband, Stephen, and son, Max.

Marsha Stopa, APP

Age: 54

Hometown: Ferndale, Michigan

As a journalist for 20 years, Marsha Stopa always figured she knew enough about a lot of things to be able to navigate her way out of any sticky spots she might encounter. That was until she became an unexpected member of the Twice Fired Club.

Stopa took advantage of the second unexpected gift of free time to reinvent herself, grabbing the chance to study and work in areas that intrigued her for years – the stock market and options trading, energetic bodywork and life coaching. Again, once she thought she knew enough to navigate out of any sticky spots, the market tanked and she found herself with more red than green on her balance sheet.

A clear sense of perspective by focusing on the important questions while surviving near-financial ruin is the real-life experience Stopa brings to her coaching and Polarity Therapy clients.

Besides being a writer, editor and life coach, she is an Associate Polarity Practitioner completing classes for the most advanced level a Polarity therapist can achieve and teaches Settling, a body-based technique to calm the nervous system. She has a Bachelor of Art in Print Journalism and Art and lives in Ferndale, Michigan.

Resources

These resources have been used and recommended by at least one of the authors. Not everything will appeal to everyone and this list doesn't include all the useful and effective resources out there by these individuals, organizations and others. We recommend you scan the list, find a title or name that resonates with you and take the next step to explore it further. Have fun!

Books

James Allen
>   *As a Man Thinketh*

William Bridges
>   *Managing Transitions: Making the Most of Change*

Po Bronson
>   *What Should I Do with My Life? The True Story of People Who Answered the Ultimate Question*

Jack Canfield
>   *The Success Principles*

Rick Carson

Taming Your Gremlin: A Surprisingly Simple Method for Getting Out of Your Own Way

Joe Caruso

The Power of Losing Control: Finding Strength, Meaning, and Happiness in an Out-of-Control World

Victoria Castle

The Trance of Scarcity: Stop Holding Your Breath and Start Living Your Life

Deepak Chopra

The Seven Spiritual Laws of Success

George S. Clason

The Richest Man in Babylon

Wayne W. Dyer

The Power of Intention
10 Secrets for Success and Inner Peace

Moshe Feldenkrais

Awareness Through Movement: Easy-to-Do Health Exercises to Improve Your Posture, Vision, Imagination®

Bernard Glassman, Rick Fields

> *Instructions to the Cook: A Zen Master's Lessons in Living a Life That Matters*

Esther and Jerry Hicks

> *Ask and It Is Given: Learning to Manifest Your Desires*

Rick Jarow

> *Creating the Work You Love: Courage, Commitment and Career*

Susan Jeffers, Ph.D.

> *Feel the Fear...and Beyond: Mastering the Techniques for Doing It Anyway*

Spencer Johnson, M.D.

> *Who Moved My Cheese?*

Byron Katie

> *Loving What Is: Four Questions That Can Change Your Life*

Daphne Rose Kingma

> *Coming Apart: Why Relationships End and How to Live Through the Ending of Yours*

Richard Miller

Yoga Nidra: The Meditative Heart of Yoga

Carolyn Myss

Anatomy of the Spirit: The Seven Stages of Power and Healing

James O. Prochaska, Ph.D., John C. Norcross, Ph.D., Carlo C. DiClemente, Ph.D.

Changing for Good: A Revolutionary Six-Stage Program for Overcoming Bad Habits and Moving Your Life Positively Forward

Don Miguel Ruiz

The Four Agreements: A Practical Guide to Personal Freedom

Don Miguel Ruiz with Janet Mills

The Four Agreements Companion Book

Douglas Stone, Bruce Patton, Sheila Heen and Roger Fisher

Difficult Conversations: How to Discuss What Matters Most

Eckhart Tolle

The Power of Now

A New Earth

James F. Twyman

The Moses Code: The Most Powerful Manifestation Tool in the History of the World

Alberto Villoldo, Ph.D.

The Four Insights

Joe Vitale

Zero Limits

Techniques

Anusara Yoga

Anusara (a-nu-sar-a), means "flowing with Grace," "flowing with Nature," "following your heart." Anusara yoga is a school of hatha yoga that unifies a life-affirming Tantric philosophy of intrinsic goodness with Universal Principles of Alignment. Learn more at www.anusara.com.

Awareness Through Movement®

The Feldenkrais Method of Somatic Education® helps people develop awareness of themselves through gentle movement sequences. Practicing this method increases your awareness of where you remain stuck in your habits, what are your limiting constraints and how to move beyond them, and how to live, think, feel and move with freedom and ease so that the impossible becomes possible. For more information visit www.feldenkrais.com

Centerpoint Research Institute

Holosync® audio technology can help you meditate deeper, reduce stress and anxiety, heal unresolved mental and emotional blocks and more. Learn more at www.centerpointe.com.

Emotional Freedom Techniques (EFT)

EFT is an emotional, needle-free version of acupuncture that is based on new discoveries regarding the connection between your body's subtle energies, your emotions, and your health. Learn more at www.emofree.com.

NLP / The Empowerment Partnership / Ancient Hawaiian Huna

Neuro-Linguistic Programming (NLP) is a behavioral technology, which simply means that it is a set of guiding principles, attitudes, and techniques about real-life behavior, and not a removed, scientific theorem. The Empowerment Partnership is the leading authority on NLP, Hypnosis, Huna and Time Empowerment Techniques, tools and techniques for the mind body and spirit. Learn more at www.nlp.com.

Polarity Therapy

A blend of modern science and complementary medicine, Polarity Therapy is a comprehensive health system involving energy-based bodywork, diet, exercise and self-awareness that is recognized by the National Institutes of Health.
www.polaritytherapy.org

The Sedona Method

Many people have used The Sedona Method to eliminate suffering and create all their heart's deepest and most worthy desires. Learn more at www.sedona.com.

Websites

The following websites offer information about additional resources and techniques that may help you along your journey.

www.Aish.com

www.AllAboutPrayer.org

www.AuthenticHappiness.org

www.BibleGateway.com

www.BuddhaNet.net

www.Chopra.com

www.cnvc.org

www.Global-MindShift.com

www.IntegralInstitute.org

www.LearningStrategies.com

www.Partnershipway.org

www.SelfGrowth.com

www.Spirituality.com

www.LemonadeNetwork.com

CPSIA information can be obtained at www.ICGtesting.com
Printed in the USA
LVOW072056281211

261434LV00001B/319/P